TEN DAYS THAT SHOOK RANGERS

Ronnie Esplin (editor)

TEN DAYS THAT SHOOK RANGERS

Ronnie Esplin (editor)

FORT PUBLISHING LTD

First published in 2005 by Fort Publishing Ltd, Old Belmont House,
12 Robsland Avenue, Ayr, KA7 2RW

Cover photographs: From top, and clockwise: Maurice Johnston and
Graeme Souness, 10 July 1989, as Johnston signs for Rangers (courtesy
of Empics); former Rangers vice-chairman Donald Findlay; stairway 13
at Ibrox stadium in the aftermath of the Ibrox disaster, January 1971;
Dick Advocaat looking pensive during a UEFA Cup tie against
Shelbourne in 1998; Alex McLeish celebrating his team's victory in the
Scottish Cup final of 2002 against Celtic (all courtesy of Mirrorpix)

Graphic design by Mark Blackadder

Printed by Bell and Bain Ltd, Glasgow

ISBN: 0-9547431-6-4

This book is dedicated to the sixty-six fans who tragically lost their lives in the Ibrox disaster on 2 January 1971, and to those who died in previous incidents in the stadium.

CONTENTS

ACKNOWLEDGEMENTS

I would like to thank my fellow contributors for their enthusiasm and effort and pay tribute to the undoubted expertise which shines through in their allocated chapters. Also, thanks to the numerous fans, former players, pundits and journalists whose input scattered throughout this book was invaluable.

To James McCarroll at Fort Publishing who came up with a compelling idea which hopefully has been brought to fruition in the way he first envisaged.

To Tom Campbell, my counterpart in *Ten Days That Shook Celtic*, who listened to and empathised with my concerns and complaints in the early stages.

Ronnie Esplin (editor), 2005

INTRODUCTION

The many and varied successes of Rangers Football Club throughout a 133-year history have been celebrated, chronicled and then embedded into the very bricks and mortar of Ibrox Stadium. As the Light Blues emerged from their humble Glasgow beginnings in 1872 to become the most powerful club in the country, rivalled only by Celtic, numerous trophies were garnered then paraded by some of the finest players in Scotland's proud football heritage and every league title or cup victory spawned its own heroes, myths and legends.

However, life at Rangers has not just been one long litany of success. The Govan club has experienced its fair share of controversial times along the way, which is where this unique publication comes in. *Ten Days That Shook Rangers* does not set out to simply eulogise the club, its players or its achievements. Instead, we shall examine and explore ten momentous events in Rangers' history which, for better or worse, helped shape, restructure or redefine one of Scotland's premier – and also much maligned – sporting institutions.

Like all the best ideas, *Ten Days* follows a simple format – ten topics are covered by ten writers who have been given free rein within their own particular chapter. The contributors are an eclectic mix of fans, historians, academics and journalists. They come from a variety of backgrounds and with varying degrees of interest in the club, ranging from the overtly partisan to the more professionally objective. It is through these differing styles and outlooks that we aim to present a book that is to varying degrees, contentious, informative, thought-provoking and humorous.

For the reader's convenience, the chapters in the book are presented in chronological order and Robert McElroy kicks us off by looking at an old fashioned, if little-known, boardroom coup involving former chairman James Bowie and legendary manager Bill Struth, which came to its rather tawdry conclusion on 12 June 1947.

Although Bowie's forced departure from Rangers at the hands of Struth was one of the most important and far-reaching developments at the Ibrox club, the significance was all but lost on the majority of supporters, most of whom were happy enough to put their faith unconditionally in the men in suits.

Bowie believed that the ageing Struth's time was up as manager but the slighted Gers boss, who had made Ibrox his own personal fiefdom, baulked at the notion and so the battle for hearts, minds and, more importantly, shareholders' votes began. The repercussions from that power struggle extend all the way to present owner David Murray. In essence, no longer would a succession of former players such as Bowie make up the board membership on a grace-and-favour basis. From this time on a new businesslike ethos would come to be associated with those who made their way up the marble staircase and out into the best seats in the house.

If some in the Ibrox boardroom of the 1940s fought tooth and nail to hold on to their positions then the same tenacity was conspicuous by its absence less than a decade later – on 14 September 1954, to be exact – when it came to defending one of Rangers' most famous players, Willie Woodburn, who was controversially banned *sine die* after only the fourth sending-off in his career.

In an innocuous early season League Cup tie against Stirling Albion, Woodburn, recovering from a knee injury, reacted to a clumsy challenge from opponent Alec Paterson with a crude head-butt. The subsequent punishment of 'Big Ben' was arguably far more brutal. Despite, or maybe because of, the Ibrox club's reputation as Scotland's 'establishment team' at that time, Woodburn never played again and was all but discarded by a club castrated by the 'dignified silence' policy that became its trademark over the years. Gavin Berry takes us through the incredible tale of the former Scotland defender's trauma after becoming the first and last Ranger to suffer the ignominy of being banned for life.

Rangers recovered from the loss of Woodburn to continue notching up domestic honours on a regular basis and were at the forefront of Scotland's challenge abroad when European club football emerged in the mid-to-late 1950s. Before Celtic had even made their competitive debut on the continent, the Light Blues had reached the semi-final of the 1960 European Cup and had been losing finalists in the 1961 European Cup Winners' Cup final.

However, the Rangers side of the early sixties, remembered by many fans and neutrals as the finest in the club's history, were beaten to the holy grail of the European Cup by their greatest rivals who famously captured the trophy in 1967.

Nearly forty years later, the shadow cast by the Lisbon Lions still looms large over Govan and given the Ibrox club's European prognosis, Rangers' hopes of lifting Europe's premier trophy may have gone for ever. But could it have been different?

Scott McDermott examines a theory held like a comfort blanket by many Gers fans of a certain age that the Light Blues could have usurped the Hoops two years earlier in the 1965 European Cup tournament but for legend Jim Baxter's cruel leg break against Rapid Vienna in the second round on 8 December 1964.

Through various protagonists of that era, McDermott examines the evidence both for and against, to evaluate just how fanciful is the notion that Baxter's Rangers could, and maybe should, have been the first British side to win the European Cup.

However, the reality was that Jock Stein and his Lisbon Lions traumatised the Ibrox club in the short term but there was still a genuine sense of shock amongst Gers fans on 1 November 1967 when they woke to discover that manager Scot Symon had been dismissed. He had survived the club's most embarrassing result ever during the previous season – the Scottish Cup third-round defeat by lowly Berwick Rangers, as well as defeat in the European Cup Winners' Cup final defeat a week after Celtic triumphed in Portugal, when he infamously played defender Roger Hynd in attack at the expense of the prolific Alex Willoughby. So it was perhaps even more surprising that the Ibrox boss was discarded when Rangers were top of the league!

Chris Williamson outlines Symon's contribution to the club and highlights both the disgraceful way in which the Rangers boss was ousted and also the curious decision to replace him with the relatively inexperienced Davie White.

If Rangers' prospects on the field were bleak at the end of the 1960s then the Govan club experienced real tragedy off the field early into the next decade. The 'Ibrox disaster', the blackest day in the Glasgow club's history, followed the Old Firm derby draw on 2 January 1971, when sixty-six fans lost their lives exiting the ground down infamous stairway 13. Sadly, it wasn't the first time needless fatalities had occurred at the stadium; the previous decade had witnessed at least three different accidents.

The disaster was a shock, but was it a surprise? How and why did it happen? And how culpable was the Govan club? In a revealing study of that distressing day, Graham Walker highlights the complacency surrounding big matches and the contempt in which football supporters were held by clubs, police and the authorities at the end of that black-and-white era. For many involved on that chilling afternoon, Walker's analysis and summation make uncomfortable reading.

The Ibrox disaster dampened down the bitterness between Old Firm fans for a short time but the traditional enmity erupted again spectacularly and most publicly after the Old Firm Scottish Cup final at Hampden Park on 10 May 1980 when hotheads from both sets of fans battled on the pitch in front of a stunned television audience. Ronnie Esplin looks back at a seminal day which not only shocked Rangers (and Celtic) but which also stunned a Scottish society that decided it was no longer prepared to ignore the often alcohol-fuelled sectarian troubles of both clubs. What were the factors involved in this unprecedented display of venom? Was it really just a conflict waiting to happen? And how did the clubs, the authorities, the police and the fans handle the aftermath? In discussing these issues Esplin concludes by asking if anything has changed in the intervening twenty-five years.

Rangers were left reeling after the Hampden riot and the club's embarrassing sectarian signing policy continued to be ridiculed as the team sunk to new depths on the pitch. It was another six years – 8 April 1986 to be exact – before the club's renaissance began under the surprising stewardship of Graeme Souness, a tempestuous Anglo-Scot who had hitherto shown little interest in club football in his own country. There have been exciting times at Ibrox in recent seasons with the capture of 'nine-in-a-row' and the recruitment of world class players like Paul Gascoigne, Brian Laudrup and Ronald de Boer but there will never again be the seismic excitement that surrounded the 'Souness revolution'.

With the initial backing of Rangers chairman David Holmes, Souness quickly imported the best of English football to help bring the championship back to Ibrox for the first time in nine years. Then, with the even more enthusiastic firepower of new owner David Murray, the Gers player-manager put in place more than a decade of almost total domestic domination. Alex Anderson – looking back to his time as an adolescent, angst-ridden Rangers fan in the 1980s – takes a sideways look at the impact of the controversial Edinburgh man and the subsequent upheaval that changed the fortunes of the Ibrox club and, indirectly, reshaped the game in Scotland.

However, if Souness's arrival in Govan caused Scottish football to gasp then his dramatic capture of former Celtic striker Maurice

Johnston on 10 July 1989, left the whole of the nation reaching for the oxygen mask. It was the day most friends and foes of Rangers said would never happen again: a high-profile Catholic playing for the Ibrox first team. Upon arriving in Edmiston Drive, the belligerent Souness had claimed he would sign anyone regardless of religion, race or colour but few believed that even he would tamper with the Ibrox club's bigoted signing policy, which had come to define the club since the first world war. However, not only did Souness sign a Catholic, he signed one who had weeks earlier pledged to sign for his boyhood heroes Celtic for the second time.

Colin Armstrong explores the most sensational signing in the Govan club's history bar none. Picking his way through the confusing chronology of Johnston's arrival, Armstrong notes the impact it had on some very entrenched ideals down the Copland Road – and perhaps more interestingly, the effect that it had at Parkhead. Armstrong claims that despite the resistance of some Rangers fans it was in fact the Celtic supporters who were most put out by a Catholic opting to ply his trade at Ibrox.

However, if Johnston's signing had blown away some dusty old practices at Ibrox, the Donald Findlay affair more than a decade later threw up age-old questions about the mindset of the Gers fans and indeed the very ethos of the club itself.

Colin Glass looks at the former vice-chairman's infamous 'karaoke session' following the Scottish Cup final on 29 May 1999, which led to the controversial Light Blues' figurehead and high profile QC, resigning from the Ibrox board.

The colourful Findlay was secretly videoed singing 'traditional' Rangers songs, one of which included the lyrics, 'we're up to our knees in Fenian blood'. The tape was sold to a tabloid newspaper that very night and in the furore surrounding the media exposé, Findlay was forced to stand down. The Govan club's reputation was damaged but their vice-chairman's reputation lay in tatters. Had anything really changed since the signing of Maurice Johnston?

Controversially, Glass, while acknowledging the complexities and anomalies that still exist amongst sections of the Rangers support with regards to their identity, makes a robust defence of Findlay. Backed by other Gers fans, Glass accuses Murray of capitulating to an anti-Rangers and anti-Protestant media that has been given carte blanche to demonise the Govan club and its supporters – and finds Findlay not guilty.

When the furore surrounding Findlay subsided – at least for a while – attention turned back to the pitch and Rangers' continuing, and frustrating, search for European credibility. Souness's big-spending strategy of the late 1980s had set the tone for the following two decades and the Ibrox club neglected its youth policy for the ready-made professionals who underpinned the successes of subsequent Gers managers Walter Smith and Dick Advocaat.

However, despite David Murray spending millions of pounds to slake the fans' unquenchable thirst for big-name players, Europe remained unconquered. Moreover, the Ibrox club's domestic success had come at a heavy price, the debt burden reaching almost cataclysmic proportions as the club entered the new millennium. The impending financial collapse in British football arguably became evident in Govan for the first time when Advocaat, the club's first foreign manager, stepped down on 11 December 2001, to be replaced by former Motherwell and Hibs boss Alex McLeish. It was a clear and unequivocal signal by Murray to even the most obstinate Rangers supporters that the big-spending days were over. Lisa Gray looks at where it went wrong for the Dutchman and just how much McLeish's controversial appointment revealed a realigning of ambitions, some of which are still to be accepted by sceptical Gers fans. Despite having seven trophies under his belt to date, including the capture of the 2005 SPL title in the most dramatic of circumstances on the final day of the season, the Ibrox boss, it would appear, is still on trial. In some ways, and perhaps unfairly, the next shock to befall the Govan club could be the day that the big Glaswegian convinces the majority of bluenoses that he really is the man to take Rangers forward.

Ronnie Esplin (editor)

1

THE DAY RANGERS BECAME
A BUSINESS

Robert McElroy

In the dark days of season 2003/04 as Rangers plunged ever deeper into a morass of debt, with the resultant debilitating effect on the team, Ibrox chairman and owner David Murray found himself the target of an escalating volume of criticism from fans and the media. When football's financial bubble burst, the Glasgow club suffered like all others and – for the first time since the steel magnate had arrived in Govan in the late 1980s – doubts over his stewardship were raised. Murray's position, however, was secure, subject only to an improbable buy-out. This contrasted with one of his predecessors some fifty-seven years earlier who, while being ousted in a board-room coup, ironically smoothed the path for Murray to assume his unassailable position.

James M. Bowie was one of the great Rangers players of the first quarter of the twentieth century, and in the second quarter was an outstanding director and chairman of the club as well as president of the Scottish Football League. Yet despite stout service to the game in general, and Rangers in particular, Bowie scarcely merited a mention in several Ibrox histories published in the fifty years following a bitterly-contested power struggle that ended on 12 June 1947. One of the club's most influential servants was unceremoniously removed not only from the chairmanship but also from the Ibrox board at the behest of manager Bill Struth. Bowie was, in all probability, never to set foot inside the stadium again before his death in 1969.

Bowie's crime was to question the ageing Struth's suitability to continue at the helm of the club and his punishment, swift and severe, had long-lasting implications down Edmiston Drive. That momentous day changed Rangers forever by ensuring that control of the great Scottish institution lay not with past service, as had been the case previously, but with shareholders who held significant port-folios, regardless of their relationship with the club. It was the day that facilitated the long journey from bluenose Bowie to business-man Murray.

Born in Partick on 8 July 1888 Bowie's early playing career encompassed Glasgow schools, Rockbank and Maryhill Juniors before turning senior with Queen's Park in 1908 where, in total, he played eighty competitive games for the Spiders. The call to Ibrox came on 6 December 1910 and Bowie made his debut in Light Blue four days later against Falkirk at Ibrox in a 1–1 league draw and almost from the outset he was a first-team regular.

Bowie was a mainstay of the Rangers team for twelve years, during which time he played 384 games for the club. He netted seventy-six goals in a successful career that saw him win five league championships, three Glasgow Cup and two Charity Cup winners' medals. In addition, Bowie represented Scotland on five occasions and in 1919 famously scored at Goodison Park against England in a 2–2 draw, converting a cross from Alan Morton, then with Queen's Park but in future years a colleague at Ibrox on the field of play and in the boardroom.

One honour missing from James Bowie's medal collection was a Scottish Cup winners' medal. Sadly his time at Ibrox, even if it did span twelve years, came right in the middle of a spell of twenty-five years (1903–28) when the club could win everything in Scottish football except the national tournament. Indeed, his one appearance in the final – against Partick Thistle in 1921 – remains the single game for which he merits a line in the history books. He was temporarily off the field of play receiving treatment for an injury, and having his shorts changed, and had to watch helplessly as John Blair netted the only goal of the game.

After an illustrious career Bowie retired in 1922, but his time at Ibrox was far from over and three years later he was invited to join the Rangers board which, as was the norm, contained another legendary former player, John McPherson. That Bowie quickly established himself as a most able administrator can be evidenced by his co-option onto the Scottish Football League management committee in 1926.

It was almost inevitable that Bowie would go to the top at Ibrox and he was elected Rangers chairman following the death of ex-baillie, Duncan Graham, in November 1934. He stood at the head of a three-man board comprised entirely of former players, with R. G. Campbell and Alan Morton being the other two members.

Bowie was appointed as a justice of the peace in 1938 and when he was elected president of the Scottish Football League in 1939, a post he would hold for seven years, the club's influence in the committee rooms and corridors of power became considerable. While at the SFL he was instrumental in the introduction of the wartime Southern League Cup and its peacetime successor the Scottish League Cup, a massively successful tournament for the first twenty-five years of its existence.

The Bowie chairmanship at Ibrox was one of almost unparalleled success: from 1934 until 1947 Rangers annexed eleven league championships including British football's first 'nine-in-a-row' which, contrary to popular opinion, was not achieved by Celtic from 1967 to 1974. Moreover, the Ibrox trophy room found room for two Scottish Cups, five League Cups, eight Glasgow Cups, eight Charity Cups, the 1940 Scottish Emergency War Cup, the 1942 Summer Cup and the 1946 Scottish Victory Cup. Even if the era did incorporate world war two the roll of honour is still an overwhelming one – yet it was an era that came to an abrupt end on that fateful June day in 1947.

The catalyst for an episode that heralded a seismic shift in the club's future arrived early in April 1947 when the chairman suggested to 71-year-old manager Struth that he should consider retirement, a request that was sugared with the promise of a seat on the board.

The proposal was certainly not an illogical one; the ageing Struth had been boss since succeeding William Wilton in 1920 and indeed had been trainer for six years before that. He had served the club through two world wars and, according to Bowie, the legendary Ibrox boss had been showing signs of strain, even if that current season was ending successfully; by its conclusion the ninth successive league championship, the inaugural League Cup and the Charity Cup had all been secured. It seemed a fitting way to end a phenomenal career and if Struth were to step aside for a younger man now, he would do so knowing his long career had ended in triumph.

The suggestion, however, was total anathema to Bill Struth. Born in the small town of Milnathort, Kinross-shire in 1875, the Ibrox boss was only three years younger than Rangers Football Club itself and such was his love for, and dedication to, the Light Blues that he lived in a flat overlooking the stadium (193 Copland Road) for the greater part of his career. The Govan club was his life; widowed in 1941, he spent long hours at the stadium (where he kept a rack of suits) sometimes returning home only to sleep. He certainly had no intention of stepping down even with the offer of a directorship as an inducement.

Bowie had also offered Struth the opportunity to name his successor but when the manager's hostility to the entire concept became clear, a compromise was floated that perhaps an assistant manager could be appointed who would, in due course, succeed to the manager's chair.

The Gers boss would later claim that, at one stage, he did offer a name to the directors but heard nothing more of it. When reading between the lines of Struth's own words – 'that gentleman has now accepted a post elsewhere in football' – two names spring to mind as to the identity of the candidate put forward. They are Ibrox legend David Meiklejohn – who early in June 1947 succeeded Donald Turner as manager of Partick Thistle – and James Scotland Symon who had recently taken up the reins at East Fife after finishing his playing career at Rangers. (Symon eventually succeeded Struth, in 1954, and in all probability had been the favoured candidate seven years earlier.)

This was not a hostile manoeuvre by Bowie. As a further conciliatory gesture by the incumbent chairman, the club's rules would be altered to suit Struth if he agreed to the compromise. If Struth remained as manager he would still become a director, a move that would require a change in the Ibrox Articles of Association, which stated that: 'No paid official of the club can join the board of directors.'

This proposal was 'harmoniously agreed' at the board meeting on 15 May, as was another change, the increase in the number of directors from three to five. The current board was comprised, as usual, of three former players – namely Bowie, Morton and George Brown. The additional two members would be Struth and club secretary William Rogers Simpson. This was, in part, recognition that there had been concern for some time over a perceived alienation between the board and the two salaried officials.

Whether the question of the appointment of an assistant to Struth had also been agreed was unclear but in any event the manager clearly felt that his position had been threatened.

The relationship between any manager and his chairman can at times be fraught but, in most situations, the advantage lies with the chairman who normally has the power of hiring and firing with perhaps his only concern being results and the reaction of the supporters.

However, in this case, Bowie had made a fatal error of judgement; he was not working from a position of strength. His own re-election as a director was approaching just two months later. In accordance with the Articles of Association, he was due to retire by rotation at the forthcoming annual general meeting, although, of course it was his intention to offer himself for re-election.

The Rangers Football Club of 1947 was a private limited company with a nominal share capital of £24,000. The club's £1 shares were trading for around £4, and the voting structure was such that shareholders holding up to five shares had one vote, with an extra vote for each additional £5 worth of shares. The balance of power obviously lay with those shareholders holding the greatest number of shares.

The annual general meeting was set for 12 June but behind the scenes moves were afoot to organise a coup that would unseat Bowie. It only came to light a few days before the meeting when many shareholders received correspondence requesting that they make available their proxy vote to Struth, secretary Simpson and the other protagonist in the triumvirate, John F. Wilson, a Glasgow councillor. (The fact that a Glasgow councillor was involved with the Ibrox club may be the most surprising aspect of the whole issue to many younger Rangers fans!)

Struth and Simpson had been busy behind the scenes and had secured the support of Wilson and other investors with substantial shareholdings. In a face-to-face meeting with the chairman, Wilson explained that his move followed an approach from 'certain interested parties'. The implications were clear. The board was set to split and Bowie's position was under threat.

An extraordinary general meeting had been called prior to the annual general meeting to ratify the proposed changes to the Articles of Association, which would see the number of directors increase from three to five. There were two sitting directors, Brown and Morton, who were safe from the subterfuge. However, standing for election were Bowie, Simpson, Struth and Wilson. There was room for three, not four, nominees. Something had to give.

A study of the share register revealed where the real power lay at Rangers. The three current directors were in place because of their outstanding past service as players, not because of their investment in shares. Bowie held just 345 shares, Morton 400 and Brown just 50. In the opposite corner stood Struth as the largest single shareholder with a total of 1,097, more than the combined total of all three directors. Wilson and Simpson held 1,043 and 744 shares respectively according to the most recent set of accounts lodged with the Registrar of Companies in 1941 (the war having suspended all requirements of company legislation). It was a *fait accompli*.

The board had little time to act, and little room for manoeuvre, but they did issue a statement condemning the move by the 'Struth faction' and calling for a meeting of shareholders at Ibrox on the evening of 11 June to discuss the matter. An appeal was also made to any shareholders who had already submitted their proxies to Struth and co to appear in person at the AGM and withdraw their support. The scene was set for an unprecedented night of drama at Ibrox and none of it was on the pitch.

As tensions grew inside the stadium, Bowie, sensing his tenure was slipping away from him, produced an impassioned speech, describing the fight as 'the most important task of my entire football career'.

In criticising the 'shroud of mystery' that surrounded the Struth faction, the chairman claimed he was also fighting for the rights of the small shareholders at Rangers, pointing out that statements outlined by the his 'enemies' laid emphasis on, 'the need to protect their financial investment'. Bowie implored the shareholders to recognise the road the club might go down when he declared: 'The club meant a great deal more than financial investment; the future of the club was to be governed either by financial interest or by loyalty and love of the team.' Fellow director George Brown understandably backed his chairman to the hilt. So did Alan Morton, absent through illness, who had sent in a poignant letter in which he asked, 'what has happened to The Spirit of Ibrox?'

A compromise proposal by one W. Gordon Bennett (himself a director in later years while at the same time a Member of Parliament) that the board be increased to six members was found to be unconstitutional as the Articles of Association stipulated a minimum period for motions to be forwarded.

Bowie knew his impending departure had nothing to do with how the club was performing. The first season of peacetime football following world war two had seen three trophies won; this meant thirty-seven trophies had been secured out of a possible fifty-seven during his tenure. Indeed, Rangers had been league champions in all but two of the thirteen seasons of the Bowie chairmanship, failing only in 1935/36 and 1937/38.

Financially, the club was also in a healthy state with profits of £12,470 in 1946/47, double that of the previous year. A dividend of 15 per cent had been declared with £6,000 transferred to the reserve fund – to finance planned ground improvements – and £5,000 to the transfer fund. No, this boardroom coup had little to do with performance and everything to do with power.

The momentous EGM/AGM of 12 June opened at 7.30 p.m. with Bowie's address to some 150 shareholders. The chairman underlined the reasons for his proposal to Struth with the simple assertion: 'He looked as if he was not standing the heavy strain.' It was, by all accounts, a bold statement to make about the Ibrox icon. Struth countered, admitting that the resignation proposal had been a bombshell, then emphasised that his shares had all been bought with money earned at Ibrox; certainly a fair declaration of loyalty.

Wilson confirmed that the move to oust Bowie was triggered by the resignation request to Struth and that secretary Simpson had also been asked to retire. He revealed Bowie had informed him earlier in the year that he would not contemplate the idea of Simpson on the board. The gloves were off and there was little dignity surrounding the occasion as the character assassinations continued. A rattled Simpson concluded the speeches by the 'Struth faction' with the vitriolic comment that Bowie did not measure up to the standards of previous chairmen.

Originally timed for a mere five minutes, the EGM went on for a full three hours. The vote of individual members showed a clear majority (84–31) in sympathy with the directors. However, a move for a card vote by Simpson – which would count total shares as opposed to an individual show of hands – showed the gloves were off. The referee between the two warring factions was the auditor, who recorded that the card votes produced a substantial majority against the board (13,286 to 3,787). The motion to increase the number of directors from three to five was carried, as was the proposal to allow salaried officials to serve on the board. It was a huge blow to the sitting board and to Bowie in particular, whose Ibrox career was now numbered in hours. It must have been disheartening for the chairman as he watched many shareholders, recognising the reality of the situation, drift away into the night.

The AGM eventually commenced at 11.45 p.m. and the bloodless coup was complete within minutes. Struth and Simpson were elected unopposed. Simpson proposed Wilson for the one remaining vacancy whilst George Brown put forward Bowie's nomination. Both motions were seconded from the body of the meeting. As before a show of hands favoured Bowie 45–27 only for the card vote to come down emphatically 13,486–2,852 for Wilson. The meeting closed at 12.30 a.m., forty-five minutes after it had begun, signalling the end of an era not just for James Bowie but also for Rangers Football Club.

Press reports were muted by today's standards and were restricted more to an account of the proceedings; there was no real analysis or recognition of the significance of the event. Nevertheless, the first step on the long road that would end with David Murray had been taken.

Struth's allies were rewarded. Simpson, who had been secretary for twenty-seven years, succeeded Bowie as chairman but died two years later. Simpson, in turn, was succeeded by Wilson, a

Conservative councillor, who was at the helm when the club entered European competitive football for the first time in 1956. Wilson died at the age of seventy-four in February 1963 and his successor was John Lawrence. Lawrence, as we shall see, provides a neat conduit between Wilson in the early days of the Ibrox club's new boardroom professionalism and the current high-powered leadership of Murray.

When The Rangers Football Club Limited was incorporated on 27 May 1899, the share capital of the company amounted to £12,000, divided into 600 proprietary shares of £5 each and 9,000 ordinary shares of £1 each. The club had continued to grow and by 1947 the share capital had been increased to £24,000. The 1899 incorporation had turned Rangers from a private club run by members who elected a committee and office-bearers (as with a golf club today) into a limited company owned by the shareholders who elect a board of directors. Baillie James Henderson was Rangers' first chairman but, on the whole, the board for the first fifty years following incorporation was heavily represented by former players: John Robertson Gow, A. B. Mackenzie, John McPherson, R. G. Campbell, Alan Morton, George Brown and, of course, Bowie.

After succeeding Wilson in 1963 Lawrence, a successful businessman who had been co-opted onto the board in 1954, quickly consolidated his power base. A decade later he held some 92,000 shares – almost all in the name of John Lawrence Glasgow Ltd – from the total share capital of 345,600. (The other major shareholders were haulage contractor Matt Taylor with 40,000, the Struth Trust with 19,000, and Peggy Morton, sister of the late Alan, who owned 5,000.)

The Lawrence era (1963–73) was one of mixed fortunes for the Light Blues. Just two league titles were secured, alongside four Scottish Cups and three League Cups. There were also two appearances in the final of the European Cup Winners' Cup in 1967 and 1972, the latter date of course bringing Rangers their first European success. He was the first Rangers chairman to see four managers in the hot seat

– Scot Symon, David White, Willie Waddell and Jock Wallace. Interestingly, current chairman and majority shareholder Murray has also gone through four managers – Graeme Souness, Walter Smith, Dick Advocaat and Alex McLeish, albeit it in a different era.

However, Lawrence was never a popular figure among the Ibrox legions and felt the brunt of criticism as the club trailed for years in the wake of Jock Stein's Celtic. The chairman appeared all too often to be away from Ibrox. He often went abroad, either on business or for a holiday, and even when he decided, after ten years in the chair, that it was time to retire, his plans ended in chaos and sparked a massive amount of bad publicity for the club.

The Ibrox chairman proposed to retire in May 1973 with the recommendation that director David Hope succeed him. At the board meeting held, as usual, in the Royal Scottish Automobile Club in Blythswood Square, Glasgow, Lawrence's proposal was confirmed by a majority vote. Opposed to the move, and resentful of Hope's sudden ascendancy, was vice-chairman Matthew Taylor who controlled 40,000 shares as opposed to Hope's 500. Taylor, a successful haulage contractor who was a lifelong Rangers fan – even driving across the Alps to watch Rangers play in Milan in 1957 – held a brief conversation with some friends and associates following the board meeting and made a telephone call to a well-known friend of Rangers who confirmed certain information regarding Hope. Taylor passed a note to John Lawrence informing him of what he had learned and reminding him of his own voting strength. The board meeting was reconvened and Lawrence was reinstated to the chair, with the agreement that he would continue as chairman until the end of that season. Hope had been chairman of Rangers for just seventeen minutes. Taylor's shareholding power was well known and would have been unlikely to have dissuaded Lawrence from stepping down on its own. So what was the big secret about Hope?

Press speculation following the turmoil of that night centred on Hope's marriage in 1930 to a Roman Catholic – who had died in

1958 – but in actual fact the information that had caused Taylor to act was that Hope himself had converted to Catholicism.

One can only speculate as to Lawrence's apparent ignorance of, or apathy towards, Hope's faith. Nevertheless, the Rangers board had retained the traditions and policies set out by their predecessors sixty years earlier in a different society. The time was not too far distant when those traditions and policies would rightly change to adapt to a new football and world order. But in 1973 the time was certainly not right – if it ever will be – for such a radical move as the appointment of a chairman from outwith those traditions.

Apart from the obvious problems surrounding Hope's religion, there were many who believed that he was not the right choice to succeed Lawrence as Rangers chairman. A self-proclaimed 'tenement boy' from Possilpark, Hope had successfully built up a chain of electrical-goods shops in Glasgow and had given the club valuable service in the creation and growth of the Rangers pools. However, his contribution to the fatal accident inquiry following the 1971 Ibrox disaster had been a great disappointment to say the least.

Lawrence's departure, however, was delayed only two months and in June 1973 he was appointed honorary president of the club, a post he would hold until his death four years' later. Taylor achieved his ambition, being elected chairman and holding the post until his death in 1975. In the boardroom reshuffle Rae Simpson (grandson of Rangers' first chairman James Henderson) became vice-chairman, and Willie Waddell and Lawrence Marlborough (grandson of John Lawrence) both joined the board.

By 1981, there had been further power shifts in the Ibrox board as businessmen jockeyed for control of the club. Marlborough controlled 96,590 shares, garage-owner Jack Gillespie 68,294 (having purchased the shares of the late Matt Taylor), taxi-magnate John Paton 12,513 and chairman Simpson owned 4,627. The board, in the main, now consisted of individual Rangers fans who had either purchased a large block of shares through income generated by a successful business – such as John Lawrence, Matt Taylor, Jack Gillespie and John Paton – or who had inherited their shareholding through a family link, such as Rae Simpson. The days of former players dominating the boardroom were well and truly over.

Clearly there remained no controlling interest at Ibrox with two distinct large minority holdings, a factor that in 1983 persuaded Alex Ferguson to decline the offer of the manager's post in succession to John Greig. Ferguson, in his book *A Light in the North*, recalled that, having been approached by Paton, he consulted former Ibrox boss Scot Symon. While urging the then Aberdeen manager to accept the job, Symon did raise the question of two separate factions on the board, a scenario that Ferguson viewed with disquiet, given his close relationship with Dons chairman Dick Donald who wielded absolute power at Pittodrie. Thus, Fergie resisted a return to his boyhood heroes and who knows how that decision impacted on Rangers' history.

Marlborough, a distant figure who had almost no affinity with Gers fans, resigned as a director early in 1983 to concentrate on his business interests in North America while retaining his large shareholding. However, Rangers were struggling on the pitch and within two years Marlborough was growing increasingly concerned at the steady drain on the finances of the Lawrence group. Accordingly, in November 1985, he reached agreement with Jack Gillespie to purchase his shareholding (by then 73,604) over the course of the next five years, acquiring 65.98 per cent of the share capital. He had effectively gained control of the club at a cost of some £920,000, although also inheriting liabilities of some £2.8 million.

Marlborough acted immediately, appointing Falkirk supporter David Holmes as his nominee on the board with the instruction to revitalise the club. Significantly, not only were some of the new Ibrox board members not former players, but also were not even Rangers fans. There were no complaints though from the disgruntled Ibrox legions as Holmes drove the 'Souness revolution', a remarkable story covered later in this book.

Rangers Football Club was now all about money. Three years later, in November 1988, the controlling interest held by Lawrence was acquired by Ayr United fan David Murray of Murray International Holdings Limited for a price of £25 per share (a total cost of almost £6 million with net liabilities of some £8 million). Murray's swoop for Rangers was proposed to him by his friend Graeme Souness, who now became a director himself, owning 10 per cent of the club. Souness followed in the footsteps of Bill Struth and Willie Waddell, who had both been the manager and a director.

The arrival of Murray was welcomed by most fans. He was by nature and inclination a supporter of the Conservative Party, a True Blue in more ways than one. His beliefs were much closer to the hearts and minds of most friends of Rangers than his predecessor as chairman, Holmes, who was a lifelong socialist. It had also for some time been no secret that the Lawrence construction empire was in financial difficulty and that one other party interested in buying control of Rangers was a certain Robert Maxwell. Murray would eventually own nearly 92 per cent of the share capital and would prove to be Souness's lasting legacy to the club. For better or worse, through good times and bad, Murray would control the destiny of Rangers Football Club for the next seventeen years and longer.

Would David Murray have control of Rangers Football Club today if James Bowie had survived as chairman in 1947? The answer is he would not, at least if the board had continued to be run by former players regardless of their financial input. But then, under such circumstances, key events such as the Souness revolution would never have happened. Had Bowie stayed on, but with Struth and Simpson as fellow directors, then the probability is that at some time in the years ahead the vested interest of those with large shareholdings would have gained a greater degree of power, although perhaps not with the same amount of bitterness.

In some respects the Bowie and Murray eras mirror each other, at least as far as success on the field of play is concerned: thirty-seven trophies from a potential fifty-seven for Bowie; twenty-six from forty-seven for Murray.

Off the field, however, the two eras are light years apart. Murray's majority control gave him absolute power as far as running the club was concerned, propelling the company into an ever-increasing spiral of debt that at one time threatened its very existence and certainly led to the catastrophic season of 2003/04. His overwhelming proxy vote ensured that he could dismiss concerns raised at one annual general meeting over liabilities in the balance sheet with a wave of the hand.

Bowie's leadership on the other hand was one of example, his position being a testament to his excellent service to the club, effectively on sufferance from the shareholders. Fiscal prudence was very much the order of the day under Bowie's chairmanship, as indeed it had been from the earliest days of the club's existence, and would so remain until 1986.

One should not judge Bill Struth too harshly, though, for the way he behaved during those stormy days in 1947. A proud man devoted to the club, Struth felt threatened by Bowie's retirement suggestion. He simply utilised his assets, and that of his supporters, to the maximum possible effect, obviously believing that there was no possibility of a compromise. Struth's ruthlessness won the day although Alan Morton and George Brown both remained on the board for many years to come: Morton until shortly before his death in 1971; Brown stepping down in 1979 when he was given an honorary directorship after fifty years of faithful service. Clearly, the loss of Bowie had not been so catastrophic for them.

Struth would himself hang on until the bitter end. His health had been failing since 1949 and a year later gangrene resulted in the loss of a leg below the knee. Undaunted, he returned to Ibrox after an absence of a few months and backroom staff would carry him up the marble staircase.

Struth finally acknowledged the need for an assistant in 1951. However, the other board members, perhaps mindful of the 1947 legacy, ignored his request. There had been growing discontent amongst the Ibrox legions and correspondence published in the *Glasgow Herald* indicated unease about the direction the club was taking and about the hierarchy running it. The unspoken belief was that, perhaps, at the age of seventy-eight, Struth should finally make way for a younger man.

However, when the manager was rushed to hospital following a fall at the end of a league game against Stirling Albion on 2 January 1954 it was all too obvious that the end of the Struth dynasty at Ibrox was nigh. On 26 January 1954 he addressed a letter to his fellow directors:

> I would like once again to bring to your notice the fact that the time has come when I feel I will have to take things easier. Could we not appoint an assistant as soon as possible with a view to his taking over the position as manager at the end of the season?

On this occasion the request was acceded to, and Scot Symon was appointed as just the third Rangers manager in the club's eighty-two-year history, to take effect at the conclusion of season 1953/54. It had almost certainly been at least one season too far for Struth; only the Glasgow Cup was secured in his final year, with the club finishing fourth in the league. Indeed, but for goal average, Rangers might have finished the campaign in eighth place, a position that would have been the lowest in the club's history. The curtain had, at last, been drawn on one of the all-time great Rangers careers, although Struth would remain a director until his death two years later.

William Struth's thirty-four years as Ibrox boss had seen domestic success unparalled anywhere in British football. Struth presided over an era when Rangers established a clear supremacy over their greatest rivals Celtic, winning twenty-five league championships, ten Scottish Cups, six League Cups, nineteen Glasgow Cups, twenty

Charity Cups, the 1921/22 Lord Provost's Rent Relief Fund Cup, the 1940 Scottish Emergency War Cup, the 1942 Summer Cup and the 1946 Scottish Victory Cup. He won a staggering 84 competitions out of 152 entered. He had the undying loyalty of all his players, past and present, until his death in 1956 and his iconic status was further underlined in 2005 when a banner was made by the Rangers supporters as a tribute for his service to the club.

However, Bowie should not be forgotten. After stepping down as a director, not long before his death in 1971, Alan Morton – still one of the most famous names in British football history – was asked as to his opinion on the best Ibrox board he had served on. His answer was immediate and emphatic: the three-man board led by James Bowie and also comprising himself and George Brown. And it should be noted that Morton had been Struth's first signing back in 1920.

Bowie, though, paid the penalty in 1947 for two errors of judgement: in making his approach to Struth just two months before offering himself for re-election; and for underestimating the power of large shareholdings. An intelligent man and, more importantly first and foremost a football man, his departure would be a considerable loss to the club, not least in the corridors of power where he had considerable influence. Bowie was sickened by the politics that had driven him away from the club he loved, and would concentrate on business thereafter as a director of Clyde Steel Structural in South Street, Glasgow; ironically not all that far from Ibrox.

However, Bowie's tussle with Struth remains one of the most significant events in the club's history. The days of former players running the club's affairs were at an end. Although in years to come Willie Waddell, Graeme Souness and John Greig did follow in the footsteps of James Bowie, George Brown and Alan Morton, they were the exception to what had been the rule.

Sadly there would never again be a former player sitting in the chair and certainly the prospect of that occurring today is remote to say the least.

There can be no doubt that the boardroom coup that skewed Bowie's place in Ibrox history also paved the way for current owner and chairman David Murray to own almost 92 per cent of the club.

On 12 June 1947, Rangers Football Club became a business.

2

AND HIS CRIME WAS TOO MUCH HEART

Gavin Berry

Sine die: two words that will forever be synonymous with Willie Woodburn. In fact, to many football fans the legendary Rangers defender *is sine die*. He defined the Latin phrase – meaning, 'without a day' – after being banned for life by the SFA on 14 September 1954 following a sending off against Stirling Albion. Quite simply, it was, and remains to this day, the most controversial disciplinary decision in the history of Scottish football.

Four Scottish league titles, four Scottish Cups, two League Cups, including three doubles and a treble, 325 games for the Light Blues and capped twenty-four times for Scotland are achievements that any footballer from any era would be proud of. Those statistics belong to Woodburn and they are what he should be remembered by.

However, unfortunately, the stigma of *sine die* will live forever with Woodburn just as, despite their success, some will always associate Eric Cantona with his kung fu-style kick on a Crystal Palace fan and Diego Maradona with his handball against England.

It's a pity because the Ibrox defender's epitaph deserves to have a far richer and more eulogistic text given the honours he picked up during a professional career spanning seventeen years.

Indeed, the defender, nicknamed Big Ben, had a song dedicated to him, which includes the lines:

> *His name was Willie Woodburn, and his crime was too much heart.*
> *He gave his all for Rangers on the field of Ibrox Park.*
> *They banished him for ever with a word they call sine die.*
> *But the name of Willie Woodburn in our hearts will never die.*

The melancholic ditty is evidence indeed of his place in the affections of Rangers supporters; certainly those of a certain vintage, some of whom even believe him to be the greatest centre half ever to pull on the famous light-blue jersey. Some of Woodburn's former team mates are equally reverential. Ibrox legend John Greig, voted by fans as 'the greatest-ever Ranger', said:

> Rangers have had some tremendous players throughout their history and Willie Woodburn was one of the very best. I used to hear people like Willie Waddell and Willie Thornton speak highly of him and that was enough to know that he was one of the best. It's a measure of how good he was that even now supporters still talk about Willie Woodburn and he should be remembered for just that – being a great player.

However, one moment of madness ruined any chance of Woodburn's name being associated with the good things in football. It came during a match against Stirling Albion on 28 August 1954 when he headbutted opponent Alec Paterson. With just seconds of a League Cup tie remaining, the Stirling player locked his legs around Woodburn's heavily strapped knee. Incensed by what he saw as a deliberate attempt to aggravate a well-documented injury that he was playing through, the Rangers defender lashed out and off he went.

Just over two weeks later, an SFA disciplinary hearing took just four minutes to come to the capricious decision and impose a ban 'without limit of time'. Woodburn, in fact, had been in the wrong place at the wrong time and was made a scapegoat as the authorities cracked down on what they saw as a general increase in on-field violence. The ban rocked Scottish football to the core. The big Gers defender wasn't the first player to receive a *sine die* suspension: Willie Kelly of St Mirren and Morton was another in the late 1940s but Woodburn was undoubtedly the most prominent and, as it turned out, the last ever in Britain. Ten years after Woodburn's punishment three Sheffield Wednesday players – Peter Swan, Tony Kay and David Layne – received life bans for match fixing after losing to Ipswich Town but their suspensions were lifted eight years' later.

Woodburn's ban was lifted three years after it was imposed but, at nearly thirty-eight, he never returned to football and the hurt felt by such a draconian sentence never left him. In an interview some thirty years later Woodburn, who passed away in December 2001, aged eighty-two, said: 'It took me a long time to recover from the ban. Nowadays players seem to get away with murder', an assertion that is even more difficult to contradict as we enter the new millennium. More than five decades down the line, and countless yellow and red cards later, it is worthwhile noting that any reincarnation of Woodburn would never be subjected to such a severe punishment. The Scottish and European courts would not permit a player's livelihood to be taken away by dint of a decision reached by a collection of self-important and amateur legislators, but that merely glimpses the point. The economics of sport, and in particular the game of football, would collapse if such a high-profile figure was so severely sanctioned for transgressions on the pitch. Indeed, such a punitive measure would never even get on the agenda of possible sanctions.

Woodburn lived to see the volatile Cantona resume his career after attacking a spectator – and this after the Frenchman had been red carded. The Manchester United striker served an eight-month suspension for that amazing tussle with an antagonistic fan, although the length of the penalty allowed him to easily remain mentally focused and physically fit until his return. Of the twenty most severe punishments in British football the former Manchester United ace is ranked fourth on a list topped by Woodburn. Other high-profile cases in that list of shame include the eccentric Italian Paolo Di Canio, who missed just eleven matches for pushing referee Paul Alcock over during a match for Sheffield Wednesday against Arsenal in 1998.

Many Gers fans point to those relatively piffling punishments dished out in England when they flag up the case of another Rangers player, Duncan Ferguson. The former Dundee United man was banned for twelve matches for violent conduct after a clash with John McStay of Raith Rovers during a game at Ibrox in 1994, which only added to the growing persecution complex down Paisley Road West. Ferguson, whose punishment was far more lenient than that of Woodburn, has never forgiven the SFA for handing him that ban. With previous off-field offences taken into account, the sullen former Ibrox striker received a three-month sentence in Barlinnie prison in October 1995. Ferguson thought a jail sentence was punishment enough and so aggrieved was he at the extra blow the SFA delivered that he announced in 1997 that he would never play for Scotland again.

However, Light Blue fans can go even further back to an incident in the late sixties involving striker Colin Stein who was involved in an incredible disciplinary case after he was sent off against Clyde. The SFA's treatment of the Ibrox club and the Scottish international that season still beggars belief. In the latter stages of season 1968/69, the Old Firm were involved in a closely contested championship race, with Celtic a couple of points clear and the two sides also due to meet in the Scottish Cup final in May. Rangers were in devastating form in the closing months of the campaign, sweeping all before them and with new signing Stein in particularly outstanding form.

However, in a league game against the Bully Wee at Ibrox in March, the former Hibs striker's world came crashing down. Rangers were coasting, 6–0 up. Stein had bagged a hat-trick but his joy was tempered when he was ordered off in the final minute of the game following an apparently innocuous incident with Shawfield full back Eddie Mulheron. Many observers believed the ordering-off to be unfair, much less the punishment that followed. The Rangers player was running down the touchline with the ball and, after several attempted kicks, Mulheron finally succeeded in bringing the Gers striker down. Stein reacted by swinging his boot, although without making contact. Both players were sent off but as there was no automatic suspensions in those days, culprits learned of their fate by appearing before the referees' disciplinary committee whose chairman at that time was Celtic chairman Bob Kelly. That Stein was suspended for an incredible six weeks – the exact length of time needed to keep him out for the rest of the season, including the cup final against the Parkhead side – still angers and bemuses Rangers fans who continue to see their club accused of receiving preferential treatment by the football authorities and officials.

There have been other examples of the Ibrox club or individual players clashing with the SFA and coming off worst. In the late 1980s controversial player-manager Graeme Souness had several high-profile brushes with the authorities during his time at Ibrox and hinted that the constant tension led to him subsequently quitting the club to manage Liverpool. So much for Rangers being the 'establishment team'.

One consequence of the SFA's treatment of the Ibrox club in disciplinary cases such as Woodburn, Stein, Souness and Ferguson is that many current Rangers fans feel their club have been victimised and some supporters even go as far as having a deliberate disinterest in the national team.

However, it will always be Woodburn's punishment that will be seen as the worst of all the perceived injustices suffered by Rangers players. Andy Bain, a well-known Rangers fan of innumerable years, even went to the SFA offices in Clyde Street on the day his hero's punishment was handed down to vent his anger. And, even with the passage of time, the veteran bluenose's disgust hasn't subsided. He said:

> I went down on the day and so angry was I that I nearly got lifted by the police. I felt so strongly about it because it was ridiculous. I was more angry because of stories I was hearing at the time which later turned out to be true. The former SFA secretary Sir George Graham revealed in his book that it was football politics that put big Willie out of the game. It's what we all suspected. The Aberdeen chairman at the time, Dick Donald, was head of the disciplinary committee and I called him for everything when he came out – to the point where the police told me to calm down. But I was just so angry. I knew Willie quite well because I went everywhere to see Rangers at that time. I spoke to him not long after it but he was never the same person again without football. Although he didn't want to show it to people, he couldn't believe the decision and he was really hurt. He didn't think he deserved it and I agree. It was ludicrous. Years later Jinky Johnstone and Willie Johnston were sent off time and again and yet Woodburn was banned *sine die* for four! In my opinion a few games would have been sufficient. He was easy to wind up during games and it had been going on for some time – it's just a pity they succeeded.

Comedian and celebrity Rangers fan Andy Cameron was lifted over the turnstile as a youngster and remembers Woodburn as one of his early heroes. He spoke highly of the defender when Woodburn was one of the first batch of twenty players to be inducted into Scottish football's new Hall of Fame. And on the decision of his indefinite ban, Cameron said: 'He was sent off just four times in his career. If they adopted the same approach nowadays the SPL would be a five-a-side league.'

However, fellow fan of that era, John Dykes, was less sympathetic:

> The ban was ridiculous but Willie was an awful silly man for what he did. It was pure madness, and incidentally the player he put the head on, Alec Paterson, was a Rangers fan. I have to say, though, that the general feeling at the time amongst unbiased football fans was that the ban was justified. It'd never happen now but in those days the SFA regime was stricter. Although I think maybe because he was a Rangers player, and the fact the Aberdeen chairman was on the committee, they decided to put the boot in. But his ban doesn't take away from the fact Willie Woodburn was a majestic footballer and we were all despondent after the decision. He was possibly the best Rangers centre half I ever watched.

Within the game, there was widespread sympathy for Woodburn from friends and foes. Celtic striker John McPhail had jousted with Woodburn on many occasions and said: 'I felt sincerely sorry for Willie. We played against each other many times, and though we battled physically for the 90 minutes, I have never known him to quibble. He could give and take.' Upon hearing the decision, the legendary Hibs striker Laurie Reilly went as far as to say: 'I'll never enjoy playing against Rangers again.' The news wasn't only greeted with astonishment in Scotland; south of the border the great Sir Tom Finney, who had crossed swords with Woodburn at international level, summed up the general amazement at the time. He said: 'We just couldn't believe it. An international player of some standing and he's been banned from the game completely? It just didn't make sense at all. There was a feeling that a grave injustice had been done. I'm sure he wasn't given the help from the people with influence.'

Woodburn's teammates were supportive. Rangers legend Ralph Brand watched his hero self-destruct that autumn afternoon and said:

> Firstly, what a lot of people don't understand is that Willie was nursing a knee injury and played with strapping on his leg. In those days you played with injuries, you didnae bloody sit the game out, you played for your cash and your bonus, or else somebody else got the money. Willie just declared himself fit and that was that. Stirling had a young centre forward [Paterson] who was obviously trying to make his mark. I was sitting in the stand and I can see the incident right in front of me even now. Willie had a few tussles with this guy during the game, and this guy was trying to be the big shot at Ibrox – playing against Rangers and Willie Woodburn. With about a minute to go they went for a ball together and Willie won the tackle, fair and square, no problem. But as he was turning to go this fella locked his legs around Willie's injured leg and of course when he went to pull away he jerked his knee and aggravated the injury. It must have been painful. But it didn't end there. On top of that the fella got up and stood chest to chest with Willie Woodburn, right in his face, giving it some lip, yap, yap, yap, yap. Willie just dropped the head. Bang. I remember the whole thing so clearly. It was right on the centre line, right in front of the stand.

Paterson, accused of provocation and still seen by many as the real villain of the piece, has kept his counsel over the years but, even half a century later, the incident still remains a sensitive issue. When I contacted him at the firm of dental technicians that he owns in Stirling, Paterson was taken aback by the phone call but still acutely aware of his notoriety. He refused to discuss the subject in any detail and said: 'If you want to know about it then check old newspapers – enough was said about it at the time. I have nothing more to say.' And with that the telephone was slammed down.

However, while Paterson slipped back into relative anonymity – a footnote to the whole affair – Woodburn's reputation was tainted forever. But it is worth setting the record straight for those who didn't see him and know only of his misdemeanour. Woodburn was sent off just four times in his career, which is no disgrace given his seventeen seasons in top-level football. He was certainly passionate about the game and about Rangers and showed that with his demeanour on the pitch. But, although no by no means a shrinking violent, to suggest he was a dirty player would be wide of the mark. A physically imposing figure, standing a shade less than six-feet tall, Woodburn was uncompromising in the tackle. Turning the other cheek, however, was simply not in his make-up and retaliation ultimately proved his downfall. The severe strictures of the *Glasgow Herald*, after a supposed friendly against Denmark at Hampden Park in May 1951, suggest that there was always in Woodburn the potential to go too far: 'We should certainly cease pointing out the continental faults of pushing and body checking' the newspaper's correspondent reported, 'so long as some of our players are indulging in more serious forms of fouling. If any of our players perpetrates such a foul as Woodburn did in the second half on Saturday, when, with a scythe-like sweep of the foot, he sent the Danish centre forward crashing to the ground after the latter had beaten him by skilful footwork, he should be dealt with appropriately.'

Was Woodburn therefore destined to clash with the authorities? He first crossed swords with the SFA in 1948 after what was described as a 'violent exchange' with Motherwell centre forward Davie Mathie. A fourteen-day suspension was incurred by the Ibrox player but it would be five years before Woodburn would find himself in trouble again; a punch thrown at Clyde striker Billy McPhail earning another ban, this time for twenty-one days. Opposing players were beginning to realise the full extent of the big defender's intolerance and even the most undistinguished players were capable of getting him to react. In a 2–0 defeat for Rangers in a league game against Stirling Albion in 1953, in which Woodburn actually scored an own goal, he was dismissed for retaliating. Rangers' former South African player Johnny Hubbard recalled that incident, which took place at Albion's old Annfield ground: 'I think it was a chap called McBain. He actually gave Willie the fisticuffs and Willie retaliated with the head. It was just a spur-of-the-moment-thing.' That third sending-off prompted the SFA to impose a six-week ban – fair enough under the circumstances – and to warn Woodburn that, 'a very serious view would be taken of any subsequent action'. It was a warning that would later come back to haunt him because, on 14 September 1954, the authorities decreed that Woodburn had transgressed once too often.

Rangers club historian David Mason explains the anomalies inherent in the SFA's corridors of power:

> It is not clear at this distance exactly who the people were who decided on the ban but in that era it is unlikely they would have had much of a football background. It would be surprising if they knew much about Willie Woodburn, what kind of man he was, or what it meant to take away a man's livelihood in that fashion. You can imagine them saying, 'This man's a hoodlum. We're going to teach him a lesson.' There was a feeling that the authorities were eyeing Woodburn, and they were looking for a chance to punish him.

Rangers manager Scot Symon, having only succeeded Bill Struth months earlier, accompanied the defender to the meeting but knew immediately the news wasn't good when the player emerged. Symon later recalled the poignancy of that moment:

When the door of the committee room opened, one look at Willie's face was enough to tell me the verdict. 'That's it all finished,' he shrugged. My own feelings were immediate. I felt as if 'The Castle' which once perched so proudly on top of the Ibrox grandstand had come tumbling to the ground around my ears.

But not everyone was convinced that Symon, a rather gentlemanly figure, or indeed Rangers as a club did enough to challenge the decision. Brand is adamant that the new Ibrox boss wasn't up for the fight as much as his predecessor would have been. He argued: 'If it had been Bill Struth that had been manager I think Willie would have remained a Rangers player. Struth was an iron man – he would have told Scottish football to away and raffle themselves, but Scot Symon was the manager and that was that.'

Despite the ban being indefinite, John Cameron QC informed Woodburn by letter that the SFA was legally obliged by a clause in its articles of association to give the player a definite date on which he may 'resume the right to play' and consequently earn money. For thirty months, Woodburn later recalled, Cameron's letter lay in his desk 'like a smouldering fuse'. He ignored it, turned instead to the men he trusted and – heavily swayed by his deep feelings of personal loyalty towards Rangers – bided his time. 'Rangers are behind you and we don't want to take it to court,' pleaded the club chairman John Wilson. But to their eternal shame Rangers were far from behind him. Two years previously, Celtic had threatened to leave Scottish football if they were to be prevented by the SFA from flying the Irish tricolour at Parkhead. Ironically, the Ibrox club had supported their rivals and the authorities backed down in the end.

Rangers had been deprived of one of their greatest servants and there wasn't a whimper of protest. If Rangers were indeed the establishment club, what benefit had accrued from being in such a privileged position?

Woodburn, of course, had no desire to go where his beloved Gers feared to tread. He later wrote:

The club had been generous to me and the last thing I wanted to do was bring it into open conflict with the SFA. I was sure that after a reasonable period the ban would be lifted. I knew my offence merited a stiff punishment but when the sentence was pronounced, words failed me completely. It was obvious I didn't have many years left at the top of football and the stigma of *sine die* was punishment enough. I had good grounds for believing that the SFA might relent after a few months. There was a top legislator who phoned me with an urgent plea not to take legal action. 'Don't do it Willie [go to court]. Things will work out for the good, you'll see.'

However, things didn't work out for the Rangers man and although Woodburn appealed to the SFA every six months, as was his right, it was to no avail. At one point, farcically, the ban was partially lifted when Woodburn was permitted any type of participation in the game – except playing. 'I know one thing,' he told highly respected journalist Hugh McIlvanney some years later, 'If I was faced with the same decision today I wouldn't hesitate for a moment to carry my fight for justice until it was lifted.'

When the SFA eventually lifted Woodburn's *sine die* ban on 23 April 1957, he was thirty-seven. It was too late. In the midst of all the appealing and protesting and hoping, Woodburn had become an ex-player. Speaking to the *Daily Record* after his suspension was lifted, he said:

I shall never play football again, not in my circumstances and I'm quite definite about that. I'm 37 years old, I haven't trained for two years, and in any case I have learned to work for my living. You can take it that reports linking me with clubs are so much nonsense. I won't play again, I don't even want to be a manager or even a scout. I made up my mind about that fully a year ago.

Asked if he was bitter, he replied: 'I used to be, but not now – although I'm very glad that the final bar has been lifted.'

True to his word, Woodburn never again became closely involved with football either as a manager or a director, and in 1979 he even turned down an invitation to stand for nomination to the board of Hearts, the team he had supported as a boy. The former Scottish international ran a garage business with his brother before going into journalism, writing for the *News of the World* for many years before retiring. His newspaper colleague Martin Frizzell recalled:

Willie remained extremely passionate about football despite a sense of injustice over his ban. His way of continuing to stay in touch with the game was to work as a columnist for the *News of the World* and he was every bit as keen on the game as he had been as a player. Willie was an educated guy – he went to George Heriot's School – but we would collaborate once a week, more to turn his thoughts into tabloid news than anything else. I wouldn't go as far as to say we were good friends but we certainly had a good working relationship and sometimes he would travel through to Glasgow and we would talk over that week's column. He would also go to a match for us and do a comment piece and I always remember him being critical of fellow centre halves and would even resort to shouting things at them. I saw, for example, Billy McNeill playing for Celtic in an Old Firm cup final and Willie would be making his feelings known in print because he'd make a mistake. He was a per-fectionist in that way and guys like McNeill and others who were the next generation in that position recognised

Woodburn as one of the greats. Willie didn't want to talk a great deal about his suspension, it was a chapter that should never have happened because his record was the same as any defender who had to go for tackles and generally go in where it hurt. Willie just got on with his life. Obviously he had his own thoughts about it and I'm sure he felt the SFA establishment which was run by some old fogies, which is the best way to describe them, who had a very limited knowledge of football. He only had four sending-offs which is almost negligible nowadays yet they threw the book at him. It was absolutely ridiculous and a lot people felt that at the time. Willie always used to point out that nobody was ever carried off as a result of one of his tackles in a match. That's what upset him most because people had this image of him in their head. In recent years I've heard average defenders described as 'Scotland's great central defenders' and it makes me laugh because I think of Willie Woodburn who was one of the greats and at a time when we were blessed with a lot of good central defenders. I'd say he was on of the top five in Britain at that time and was a Scotland international for most of that period along with his Rangers teammate George Young who, along with Bobby Evans of Celtic, were the backbone of the Scottish team. I remember the great Tom Finney and Jackie Milburn (who was almost God in Newcastle) were also working for the *News of the World* at that time. When we used to have Christmas functions and other social nights the three of them always got on like a house on fire, despite having been great rivals during Scotland–England games. Everyone respected him, even Celtic supporters. I'm sure a lot of older Celtic fans to this day still admire him.

However, it should be remembered that Woodburn's career was truncated, not still-born. Born on 9 August 1919 in Edinburgh – at 164 Gorgie Road to be precise – he attended Heriot's Grammar School, where rugby, not football, was the preferred sport. However, football was Woodburn's passion and he joined a local junior club called Edinburgh Ashton before moving on to Musselburgh Athletic and Queen's Park Victoria XI. The 'real' Queen's Park from Glasgow gave him a couple of trials but nothing came of them and when he walked through the gates of Ibrox for the first time as an 18-year-old in October 1937 – on a wage of just £4 a week – he was immediately a Rangers man.

Woodburn, working as an apprentice plasterer, made an almost instant impact and on 20 August 1938 he made his first-team debut in a 2–2 home draw with Motherwell. The teenager held his place for eight consecutive league games – even surviving a 6–2 mauling at Celtic Park on 10 September – before veteran international Jimmy Simpson returned to the team. Far from being a prototype bruiser, in his early days at Rangers the sinewy, beautifully balanced Woodburn was criticised for dallying on the ball too long when really all manager Bill Struth wanted was a human brick wall. 'You've got this juvenile habit of holding the ball in the penalty area and inviting trouble,' Struth told Woodburn after the 19-year-old's first Old Firm derby had ended in heavy defeat for Rangers, 'all we expect of you here is that you clear your lines. Leave the wing-halves to play the football.'

Thus, most of the remainder of that first season was spent in the reserves but Woodburn did come back at the campaign's climax as Rangers wrapped up another title triumph. The Charity Cup was the traditional end-of-season competition and the young centre half duly secured his first winner's medal when the Light Blues defeated Third Lanark 7–4, bizarrely on corners, following a scoreless draw at Hampden Park. Woodburn had done enough to be considered the first-choice pivot at the start of the following season but that was the summer of 1939/40 and for the next seven years his career – like countless others – was severely disrupted by world war two. During the war, when Rangers were allowed to field two teams, Woodburn largely played in the lesser of them but he was clearly a force for the future.

As it transpired, the earlier post-war years saw the central defence position go to big George Young, a player with a sharply contrasting style: tall, heavily built and with a more basic element to his play. The selection problem was resolved when Young moved to right back following the retirement of Dougie Gray, enabling Woodburn to take his place at centre half. And, with other accomplished Scottish international defenders like Shaw, McColl and Sammy Cox, Rangers embarked on a long spell of domestic success.

Woodburn became well-liked by the Ibrox fraternity who christened him 'Big Ben', not, as you might expect, in tribute to his size and reliability but as a result of his impassioned and prolonged celebration of a Gers victory over Benfica in Lisbon during the late 1940s. Woodburn insisted on raising his glass every few minutes and bellowing: 'Viva Benfica!' His chant continued through the night and into the next day and the Rangers players felt his performance merited some kind of permanent commemoration. So Big Ben it was.

However, unlike the meticulous clock that towers over Westminster, Woodburn was thought to be ahead of his time as far as his style of play was concerned, a *libero* before the phrase was even invented. The late Rangers striker Alex Willoughby commented some years after Woodburn's heyday:

Willie was a guy that could have played in the modern game because not only could he play, he was also a guy that could organise and talk and when you play at centre back that's crucial. If you read the game well and talk well, you save your legs and Willie was that sort of player.

Ralph Brand added:

Willie had everything. Apart from being one of the hardest men, he was also one of the most cultured centre halfs in the country. He could bring the ball down, or he could clear it, or he could head a first-time ball to the likes of Sammy Cox. He played it with skill which was rare because in those days centre halfs were all-out stoppers. But Willie made you play too, because if you didn't he just ran over the top of you.

Another Ibrox legend, Eric Caldow, reiterated the sense of esteem in which Woodburn was held by his teammates:

My first-ever game for Rangers was at Ibrox in September 1953 against Ayr United, a year before Willie's final game and he made his presence felt right away. I went for a ball with him and he shouted, 'That's my ball.' But it was too late – I got in his way and when he got the ball I went with it. He was that kind of player, on the ground or in the air he took the lot – man, ball, everything. He wasn't dirty but he would have gone through a brick wall for Rangers, and always encouraged us young players to do the same.

Woodburn was also versatile and Bill Struth used him at wing half, inside forward and even centre forward on occasion. He scored just two goals for Rangers, one in a 5–1 home league win over St Mirren on 12 August 1939 and the other over a decade later at Fir Park in a 3–2 win over Motherwell on 7 April 1951.

In April 1947, Woodburn made his international debut at Wembley in the annual encounter with England. He won twenty-four caps in all, the first three in that same season, and five of them in classic confrontations with the Auld Enemy. Had Scotland not obstinately refused to take part in the 1950 World Cup, for which they qualified, he would certainly have played for his country at the finals in Brazil.

It wasn't until 1949, though, that the famed Ibrox 'Iron Curtain' defence of Brown; Young, Shaw; McColl, Woodburn and Cox came together as a regular unit, their level of consistency and perform-ance perhaps unmatched in the half-century that has since passed. Woodburn was an integral part of the Rangers team that won the very first treble in 1948/49 and captured three successive Scottish Cups from 1948 to 1950.

One person who knew Big Ben as a man better than most was Willie Waddell, Woodburn's friend and teammate with Rangers and Scotland. Years after Woodburn's departure from the game, Waddell said:

> He was always a fierce competitor, but I think that basic determination was distorted by the mystique of Rangers. There is no doubt that in our time the very act of pulling that blue jersey over your head did something to you. All the talk about tradition, about the privilege and responsibility that went with being a Rangers player definitely had its effect. I think Willie felt it more than any of us. I am sure that obsession with winning for Rangers had a lot to do with his troubles. Still, it would be absolutely ridiculous to think of him as maliciously violent. You couldn't meet a more likeable, gen-erous man. He could be wild but when I was best man at his wedding I had to hold his hand through the ceremony!

South African Johnny Hubbard remembers 'one or two incidents' soon after the war when Woodburn simply snapped rather than face up to the realities of defeat, as he recalled:

> He actually threw his boots through a window at Hampden after we lost a Scottish Cup semi-final there. He just lost his head. I mean, I'm sure he didn't actually know what he was doing but he did it all the same. He was so passionate about

Rangers, we all knew what he was like. Sadly, in 1954, the rest of the country had also come to realise the full extent of the big defender's intolerance. Willie already had a touch-paper temper and that year he lit the spark. It had been coming for some time.

Big Ben was an Ibrox hero who earned his rightful place in the club's Hall of Fame. However, the big defender paid the ultimate price for his moment of madness by receiving a *sine die* suspension. And sadly, that will remain the legacy of Willie Woodburn, Rangers and Scotland.

3

MILAN MAESTROS?

Scott McDermott

The Milan Maestros. Nice ring to it, eh? It's the headline or catch-phrase every Rangers fan dreamt about in season 1964/65 when many bluenoses believe *they* should have been in Italy's fashion capital on 27 May that year to witness the Ibrox club lifting football's most prestigious piece of silverware in Internazionale's own back yard. Instead, Inter defeated Benfica 1–0 in the San Siro that night and Rangers' quarter-final challenge was just a distant memory to the Italians. But for some Gers fans, the notion that an opportunity to become the first British team to win the European Cup had been lost that year has never been forgotten. And central to that flight of fancy is Jim Baxter, arguably Rangers', and indeed Scotland's, greatest-ever player.

Reminiscing about former or potential glories is permitted in football; it's all part of the fun of being a fan and it can also give supporters something to hang on to, something to argue about in the pub or tell the grandchildren. And Rangers' European campaign of 1964/65 inspired by the legendary Baxter, who tragically broke his leg against Rapid Vienna, falls into that category. But for that twist of fate, according to some strands of Ibrox folklore, Scottish and European football history could have been oh so different.

Even now, the words 'Lisbon' and 'Lions' stick in the throats of some of Rangers' most ardent followers and that's not entirely down to the traditional rivalry between themselves and Celtic. It isn't just the Parkhead side's success in Lisbon's Estadio da Luz in 1967 – ironically against Inter Milan – that irks Rangers fans, it's the fact that the Ibrox men could and maybe should have won that trophy first. As it was, the Light Blues, at their peak in domestic terms, lost by a solitary goal (3–2 on aggregate) to the great Italian side in the quarter-finals of the competition two years earlier. And their chance of attaining the same legendary status the Lisbon Lions subsequently achieved was gone. The 'Milan Maestros' headline never saw the light of day.

One of the most pivotal moments in the Ibrox club's history occurred in the previous round when Baxter, Rangers' one and only genuine world-class player at that time, sustained a broken leg against Rapid Vienna. With just twenty seconds remaining in Austria's Prater stadium – later to become better known as the Ernst Happel stadium – 'Slim Jim' was crocked by a man many Gers fans insist wrecked their European Cup dream. Right half Walter Skocik, who had been given a torrid time by the mercurial Scotland midfielder, made sure he had his revenge with a crude challenge which immediately and dramatically changed the fortunes of the Glasgow club both at home and abroad.

Sure, the Light Blues went on to win the European Cup Winners' Cup in 1972 but from 8 December 1964, when Baxter writhed in agony on the Austrian turf, not only were Rangers' European hopes that season demolished but also the Ibrox side didn't play in club football's premier competition again for a decade. Jock Stein's arrival at Parkhead the same season heralded a golden era for Celtic – they won nine league titles in a row in addition to their great night in Portugal. But there's also a valid argument that the Parkhead side would not have had such a clear run at their nine-in-a-row era if the Fifer had remained in Govan.

If anyone is still in doubt about Slim Jim's quality or the effect he had on Rangers, they only need to look to his domestic record at the club: he played in eighteen Old Firm derbies and lost on only two occasions; an incredible statistic. Baxter also appeared in seven domestic cup finals during his five-year stint and was never on the losing side. Those figures speak for themselves and therefore one could legitimately ask, would Celtic have been given the chance to take part in the European Cup campaign if Baxter had been at Ibrox?

However, Baxter no doubt had other things on his mind as he lay prostrate in Austria that fateful night. Skocik's tackle ruled him out of action for three months and when he returned he never quite got back to his inimitable best, even though some would argue that his virtuoso performance at Wembley against England in 1967 was the finest display of his career. But by then the big Fifer had moved on to Nottingham Forest, after an ill-fated spell with Sunder-land. In truth, Baxter's genial mocking of the world champions provided only a fleeting glimpse of what he was capable of at that time and his consistency level had dropped considerably after leaving Ibrox. And it's widely accepted that his return to Glasgow in 1969 was as mistimed and ill-advised as Skocik's challenge in Vienna.

Baxter's influence on that Rangers side of the early sixties is unquestionable. The effect Slim Jim had at Ibrox wasn't lost on his great Old Firm adversary, but close friend, Billy McNeill. The captain of the Lions – who went on to manage the Parkhead side twice – remains highly complimentary about Baxter:

Baxter gave Rangers the quality and class that very few teams had at that time. When he broke his leg in '64 it must have been a massive loss to the club. Jimmy could have played anywhere in the world in my opinion. Any club who wanted a classy, constructive playmaker should have signed him – he would have added volumes to their side with his ability. He would have loved facing the Italians that year, really loved it because the bigger the occasion the more he enjoyed it.

Everyone connected with Scottish football during that era accepts Baxter was at his peak around 1964. That famous Rangers line-up; Ritchie, Shearer, Caldow, Greig, McKinnon, Baxter, Henderson, McMillan, Millar, Brand and Wilson still rolls off the tongue of Ibrox fans, some of whom weren't even born during that era. That's always a decent barometer of just how good a football team were. It was on 16 September 1962 that this famous eleven were first given an outing and they are still held in admiration by Rangers fans today even though some subsequent Ibrox sides have been equally successful.

But Baxter was the lynchpin. His inclusion in the Rest of World team that faced England at Wembley in 1963, confirmed his world-class status. Not that he had any doubt about his place in the game. He once said:

> I never practised football in my life – never. Everything that happened to me was natural. Jimmy Johnstone told me about how he used to practise by dribbling round milk bottles but I didn't need to do that. The only thing I ever practised was jookin' up and down to the bookies to put a line on. The bigger the team, the better I played, the bigger the occasion, the better I was. Everybody would be sweating their bollocks off but I was in my prime during that period.

When Baxter arrived at Ibrox from Raith Rovers in 1960, he made an immediate and startling impact. Strikers Ralph Brand and Jimmy Millar were now getting the quality of service from midfield they required. Brand finished Gers' top scorer with twenty-four goals as they went on to win the championship and League Cup double in season 1960/61.

The introduction of the gangly youngster also signalled a change in Rangers' style of play. During the post-war era they were regarded as a physical outfit, equipped with brute strength rather than natural, football ability but he had given the Govan club a certain finesse and elegance; his knack of unlocking defences with his left foot was priceless to Scot Symon's side.

In Baxter's first full season, Rangers reached the European Cup Winners' Cup final after seeing off Ferencvaros, Borussia München-gladbach and Wolves but in the final against Fiorentina, the Italians were simply too good and the Light Blues lost out 4–1 on aggregate.

However, Rangers' successful new style was punctuated by heavy defeats from some of Europe's top sides. In late April and early May of 1960, six weeks before Baxter's arrival, they were trounced 12–4 on aggregate by Eintracht Frankfurt in the semi-final of the European Cup. Although, technically, the Ibrox men were just one tie away from the final, in reality they were light years away and still had a lot to learn. The Germans went on to the final at Hampden Park but themselves were taught a lesson by Real Madrid in one of football's most memorable matches.

Respected sports journalist Bob Crampsey remembers that period well, in particular Rangers' defeat at the hands of the Germans. He said:

Rangers were taken seriously in Europe at that time but they still suffered some heavy beatings along the way. Eintracht Frankfurt beat them 12–4 on aggregate and later on Real Madrid also beat them 7–0 over two legs (in the 1963/64 European Cup). I remember coming away from the Eintracht game thinking any team taking twelve off Rangers has to be the greatest side in the world. But Real chewed-up Eintracht and spat them out at Hampden. Rangers learned from it and were certainly better equipped in '64/65 for a good run in Europe and Baxter was good enough to play in the company of teams like Inter Milan. In many ways he'd have been better suited to play on the continent than in Scotland and in that sense he was ahead of his time.

In 1961/62, Scottish champions Rangers were knocked out of the European Cup by Belgian side Standard Liege, losing 4–3 on aggregate at the quarter-final stage and, the following season, the Ibrox club's European involvement ended with an 8–4 aggregate defeat by Tottenham Hotspur in the Cup Winners' Cup, the Londoners going on to lift the trophy.

Despite the feeling that Rangers were slowly becoming a force in European football, their annihilation by the mighty Madrid in September–October of 1963 badly affected Baxter. The proud Fifer was embarrassed by the result:

> Europe was something we never quite conquered in my five years at Ibrox. That was a great disappointment to me. The year I broke my leg they said it was our best chance ever but for most of the time we didn't plan for it properly. We would play against Inter Milan the same way we'd play against Partick Thistle or Third Lanark. We didn't change anything; but you can't do that in Europe.

Not that Baxter locked himself in the house in self-pity after the two defeats by Madrid. This is evidenced in the almost surreal anecdote he told involving the legendary Ferenc Puskas, who scored the only goal of the game in the first leg at Ibrox. In *Puskas on Puskas*, edited by Rogan Taylor and Klara Jamrich, Baxter revealed he took the portly little striker into the city's George hotel before they ended up at a house party in Drumchapel where Puskas had what is euphemistically called a 'romantic liaison' with one of the local girls in the scullery.

However, the drubbing from Madrid was, in fact, a Euro wake-up call for boss Symon, Baxter and Rangers. In 1964/65 – after winning back the league title from Dundee the season previously – they once again entered the European Cup, knowing their style of play and level of performance had to change if they were to realise their potential.

The campaign started off with a comfortable 3–1 home win over Red Star Belgrade in the preliminary round but, once again, their away form almost put them out of the competition. In Belgrade the Yugoslavs led 4–1 before defender Ronnie McKinnon's crucial goal levelled the scores on aggregate. Under today's UEFA rules, Rangers would have gone through on away goals but instead they had to settle for a play-off at Highbury in north London.

On Arsenal's ground Rangers finally looked like a team capable of mastering European football. Inspired by Baxter the Scots won 3–1, thanks to a Jim Forrest double and another by Brand. It was a mature victory for the Scottish champions; they destroyed Belgrade that night and went into the next round with Rapid Vienna high on confidence.

However, in the first leg at Ibrox, the Austrians proved a stubborn side and Rangers could only breach their defence once. Typically, Baxter was involved; his measured pass inside their right back Hoeltt found Davie Wilson and the left winger made no mistake with his finish past the Vienna keeper, Veres. But it was a slender lead and, judging by Rangers' recent results in Europe, many pundits felt they had lost their chance of progressing. Despite adverse weather in Vienna – soldiers had to be deployed to shovel snow off the pitch – the game went ahead on a sodden Prater pitch, ironically, where Inter had captured the European Cup against Real Madrid the season earlier.

Baxter, as captain, knew his side would have to adapt to the difficult conditions:

They could play offside all night without breaking sweat so

there was no point in us running about daft on a pitch like that. They were at us right from the start and it took us about twenty minutes to get past them. I got the ball and I had to hold on to it to make sure our lads stayed onside. It took a wee while – I beat three of their players while I was waiting – and then I spotted Jim Forrest. They were quick to come out so the ball to Jim had to be quicker. But I got it to him and he scored – that put Rapid in real trouble.

Now leading 2–0 on aggregate, Rangers were in easy street and began to revel in the Scottish-like conditions. Baxter recalled:

We went one-up and they couldn't cope with us – we really were enjoying ourselves. Skocik must have had the worst night of his career. I just kept nutmegging him. I don't know how many times I put the ball through his legs but it must have been dozens – I lost count. Every Rangers player was on song that night. I'll tell you how good we were – the Rapid supporters were throwing snowballs at their own players and cheering us. We were just thinking about who we'd get in the next round and the way we were playing we didn't care who we got. The game was a doddle for us and all I remember thinking about is that we had a party on later that night. I knew there wasn't long to go so I started to walk towards the dressing rooms.

Baxter's arrogance, though, would come at a price. Little did he know that, with just seconds remaining, his European adventure was coming to an end.

He vividly recalled what happened next:

Something happened near me so I turned round and asked for the ball. The next thing I knew – whack! Skocik hit me from behind and broke my leg. I don't think he meant to do it even though I'd given him a roasting all night. If it had been him against me I'd have kicked me much sooner – I was in scintillating form that night.

But I knew my leg was broken – I heard it break. Davie Kinnear ran on and I said to him 'fuckin' leave it alone'. He was the type that would have just grabbed it when he came on so I said 'fuckin leave it, d'ye hear me?' Then I saw Scot Symon coming on and I said, 'it's broken boss'. He said, 'My God, you sure?' I says, 'Aye I'm sure, a'right.'

Robert Hendry from Glasgow has been a season-ticket holder at Ibrox for twenty-five years and was in Barcelona's Nou Camp stadium on Rangers' greatest-ever European night when they defeated Dynamo Moscow 3–2 to lift the Cup Winners' Cup in May, 1972. Hendry is in no doubt about the impact the talismanic playmaker's injury had on the club and its supporters:

Baxter had so much class. He wasn't a workhorse and his right leg was for standing on but his ability was unbelievable. He had so much self-belief and arrogance to go with it. He could have gone in against any player in the world and it wouldn't have fazed him. Put it this way, he was the only player in Scotland at that time who could have held his own against the likes of Inter Milan in that quarter-final. Their reputations would have meant nothing to Baxter, whereas some others might have been overawed. He would have looked on it as his perfect stage – he feared nothing in a football sense. The fact he wasn't there for the game was a major blow for the rest of the Rangers players. A lot of them looked up to him and if they ever wanted rid of the ball he was the man to take it off them. He was the get-out for other players who didn't have the skill Baxter had. Players like

Greig or McMillan would never win games for you but Baxter was the Rangers match winner and against Inter we lacked creativity going forward. There was a general feeling amongst the Rangers support that his leg-break was costly for us. A lot of fans were convinced if he was available we might have won it. We lost narrowly and Baxter might just have made the difference.

Baxter returned to the team hotel that night in Salzburg, apparently unflustered by the injury and Rangers' diminished hopes in the competition. Room service was ordered by friends; champagne, brandy, Black Label, ice and two fillet steaks. Another visitor arrived at Baxter's room – she left in the morning. A friend later commented: 'Typical Jim – one leg broken and he still managed to get the other one over.'

However, there was an element of bravado in the midfielder's relaxed manner. Journalist Rodger Baillie – who was Baxter's best man at his wedding in 1965 – was in the Austrian hotel that night and says: 'I remember Jim was extremely cavalier and matter-of-fact about it. Most people would have been in tears but Jim just saw it as a minor setback. Deep down though, he knew it was a major setback and he was gutted. He was remarkably resilient in situations like that.'

The hosts seemed to appreciate they had been in the company of genius. Franz 'Bimbo' Binder, Rapid Vienna's joint coach, said afterwards: 'We were not just beaten by a fine team but a truly world-class player in Jim Baxter.' It was high praise indeed from another football legend. Binder remains the only European to have scored more than one thousand career goals. The match commentator on Austrian television was also blown away by the Gers star's performance; he said Baxter was the 'best player Austria had seen since Pele'.

The Scottish press recognised the enormity of the Ibrox side's loss. The *Daily Record* carefully juxtaposed their two stories the following morning – the match report headed in bold by 'Triumph', while opposite the picture of a dejected Baxter on a stretcher underneath the word 'Tragedy' summed up the game's ending. Journalist Hugh Taylor wrote: 'Jim Baxter was only seconds away from his greatest triumph . . . Baxter had been the architect of Rangers' famous victory. . . . The Baxter leg break was a sad end to a gallant Rangers performance.'

Nonetheless, Rangers were drawn against a star-studded Italian side that included greats like the marauding Giacinto Facchetti at left back, the stylish Aristide Guarneri at centre half and the great Sandro Mazzola in attack. But the team's talisman was Luis Suarez, then the world's most expensive player, having been signed for £200,000 in 1961 from Barcelona. Suarez was incomparable, a true genius; he had been chosen as European player of the year in 1960 and had inspired the Spain team that won the European Championship in 1964. It was therefore hardly surprising that Inter, under the guidance of their legendary manager Helenio Herrera, were the current European Cup holders having ended Real Madrid's dominance of the tournament by beating them 3–1 in the final with Mazzola scoring twice. The Italians then went on to prove they were the best team on the planet by lifting the Intercontinental Cup after defeating their South American counterparts, Independiente of Argentina. Inter also had the notorious *catenaccio* defence – the stingiest rearguard of all time. And, to cap it all, Rangers would be without their best player.

The first leg was scheduled for 17 February 1965 and the teams that took the field in front of 49,520 fans in the San Siro were:

Inter: Sarti, Burgnich, Facchetti, Tagnin, Guarneri, Malatrasi, Domenghini, Mazzola, Peiro, Suarez, Corso.

Rangers: Ritchie, Provan, Caldow, Wood, McKinnon, Greig, Henderson, Millar, Forrest, Brand, Wilson.

Without Baxter, the Govan side's task was difficult enough but when Lady Luck went missing as well then the improbable became impossible. Rangers lost three goals in three crazy minutes, two of them in very unlucky circumstances; one a deflected shot past Billy Ritchie and another that ricocheted off the head of Jimmy Millar into the path of Suarez who netted easily.

The Scots composed themselves and battled on but, even when Jim Forrest pulled a goal back to make it 3–1, the Ibrox fans knew their side faced an uphill task in the second leg in Glasgow. For the return match – in front of 77,206 at a snow-bound Ibrox – Inter made two changes; Corso and Malatrasi dropped out, with Picchi and Jair coming in. For their part Rangers left out Wood, Brand and Wilson to bring in Hynd, McLean and Johnston. Scot Symon's men got off to a great start. Forrest scored within six minutes but the well-drilled visitors remained calm and, apart from a George McLean shot that came off the crossbar, the Scots' chances were limited. It was a 1–0 victory on the night but Rangers were out 3–2 on aggregate.

The Ibrox club would live to fight more battles on the continent but Baxter would never play for Rangers in Europe again. When back to full fitness, the troubled Scottish international became embroiled in a dispute with the club over wages. He felt insulted by what they were offering him. The board's attitude at Ibrox was that no player was bigger than the club – even Baxter – and every first-team member would be on the same wage.

No exception would be made, even for an exceptional player and in May 1965 Baxter was transferred to Sunderland for £72,500, four times what Rangers paid Raith Rovers for him five years earlier. However, the former miner from Hill O'Beath saw his career go into a rapid decline down south, especially when he moved on to Nottingham Forest for £100,000 in 1967. He would return to Rangers two years later, a shadow of the player he once was. Tragically, the Fifer quit football at the age of thirty and only lived for a further twenty-six years. In 1994, doctors told him if he didn't quit drinking he would die. Typically, Baxter replied: 'Ach, I'll gie it a year and see how it goes.' Despite a successful liver transplant, he died on 14 April 2001.

In the mourning that followed the death of a Rangers great, the argument again returned to the early sixties and Baxter's hey-day. Could this wayward genius have brought the European Cup home to Ibrox two years before Celtic? Of course, it's a hypothetical argument and it's impossible to say for certain whether Slim Jim had so much control over that Rangers team in 1964 that he could have single-handedly inspired them to victory over Inter. And even if he had helped them overcome one of the most formidable club sides in the history of the game, there was still a semi-final and final to be won.

Baxter himself once recalled the bittersweet experience of Vienna:

Rangers had grown up in Europe and I always felt we'd win in Austria. Looking back, I think that game was the best I ever played for Rangers. Not because I played well – which I did – or because I broke my leg but it was the best team performance we produced in my time at Ibrox. People said after Vienna that we could go on and win the European Cup and I do think it was the best chance we ever had of winning the competition.

Celtic legend Billy McNeill is genuine when he says:

That Rangers team in the sixties were a smashing side, undoubtedly. With Baxter they were even better. Without him, they suffered a real loss. My abiding memory of Jimmy is his overall ability. All he wanted to do when Rangers were in possession was get a hold of the ball. He wanted to attack and hurt the opposition – his passing, dribbling, everything was just fabulous. There's no sense in presupposing about these things – it's hypothetical and who knows if they could have gone on and won the European Cup. No-one can speak with any real authority on that. All I know is, when Baxter got injured it was a major blow to Rangers because he was such a good player.

Ironically, and perhaps surprisingly, Eric Caldow – one of Rangers and Scotland's most decorated players – isn't as forthcoming in praise of his former teammate:

That team in the sixties was one of Rangers' best. We all had a job to do in the team and we did it well, that's why we were successful. I remember when Jim broke his leg, it was a huge blow to us. At that time, a leg break was a very serious injury. It was probably the best team I ever played in and we felt confident of winning every game that year, even against the Europeans. Jim was his own man, a great player obviously and my job was just to get the ball to that left foot of his. But you have to remember that although Jim was an individual, it was a great team effort from us. In my opinion we had better players than Jim in the team at that time. He was a fantastic player but the rest of the players didn't have to look up to him in any way – we had some great footballers in the side.

The likes of Willie Henderson and Ronnie McKinnon were excellent players in their own right. Jim was an attacking wing-half but he was slow, couldn't tackle and had no right foot. That's a fact. Jimmy Millar said to me recently he was surprised Jim was named in the greatest-ever Rangers team. I must admit when we gave him the ball, he was terrific and his left foot could do great things. But he isn't the best player I've seen at Ibrox – George Young, Sammy Cox and Ian

McColl were three above him for me. We knew we could have won the European Cup before Celtic but there's no point looking back and regretting anything, including Jim's injury.

Rodger Baillie, who knew Baxter better than most, insists Rangers could have lifted the trophy if it weren't for Slim Jim's absence:

Jim was vitally important to the Rangers team in '64. You only have to look at how it all went pear-shaped when he was out injured. He was out from December until March and they didn't win the league that year – they were fifth and then they didn't win the league for another ten years. Before the leg break Baxter was at his peak and I don't think he ever reached those heights on a consistent basis again.

There was the odd occasion like the '67 match at Wembley but he left Rangers and never really got back to his best. Although they got to the semi-final before, it was possibly Rangers' best-ever chance of winning the European Cup during that era – Inter only just beat them in the end. Symon was desperate for him to play in the second leg at Ibrox but he missed it – he played three days later at Easter Road against Hibs in the Scottish Cup. Rangers were the holders but they were beaten 2–1 and ironically enough it was one of Jock Stein's last games as manager of Hibs. On that day, 3 March, they announced he was going to Celtic. It's impossible to say whether Rangers would have won it; I'm really not sure but Inter went on to win it so that shows just how close Rangers were to getting their hands on the trophy.

Perhaps in a more contemporary Old Firm scenario we can try and assess Baxter's importance to Rangers by comparing it to Henrik Larsson's influence at Celtic. It's not bold or rash to say that the Swedish striker was as important to Celtic as Baxter was to Rangers.

In 1999, Larsson suffered a broken leg in two places during a European tie against Lyon and Celtic were knocked out of the competition by the French side 2–0 on aggregate. They also went on to lose the league title to Rangers by a massive twenty-one points in the Swede's absence. Up until that horribly graphic injury, Celtic's top marksman had rattled in twelve goals by October of that season and he would go on to become one of the greatest strikers in their history.

Larsson made a full recovery and returned to play an integral role in their journey to the 2003 UEFA Cup. He scored the decisive or winning goal for Celtic in six of those matches, including strikes against Liverpool, Blackburn Rovers and Celta Vigo. He also notched the only goal of the game in the second leg of the semi-final against Boavista, a goal that sent Celtic and an army of supporters to Seville for the final. Even in defeat – they lost 3–2 to Jose Mourinho's Porto – Larsson headed both Celtic goals.

Like Baxter to Rangers, the Swede's influence was invaluable to Martin O'Neill's team. The talismanic striker was the one player who could win the match on his own, albeit in a different manner to his Ibrox counterpart. Larsson left Glasgow in the summer of 2004 and Celtic still haven't recovered from his departure. The Swede hit 242 goals in his time at the club – 44 in one season – and so far has been irreplaceable.

Robert Hendry, who has seen both Baxter and Larsson in the flesh, believes it's fair to compare the two Old Firm icons. He said: 'You can definitely draw a comparison between Larsson and Baxter – two totally different players but with a similar influence on their teams. It was incredible the amount of times Larsson got Celtic late goals, crucial goals and they just don't have that now.' Celtic great McNeill agrees, saying: 'It was the equivalent of Celtic losing Larsson recently. It was as big as that and a very similar problem.'

If Rodger Baillie perhaps erred on the side of optimism when assessing Rangers' chances of European glory in 1965, then Bob Crampsey has his doubts as to whether the Light Blues would have defeated Inter Milan; even with Baxter in the team. However, Crampsey admits he also called it wrong three years later when, like many other Scottish football observers, he didn't believe Celtic had the quality to go all the way and lift the trophy in Portugal. Crampsey said:

> Baxter was exceptional. He couldn't head, tackle or kick with his other foot but Stanley Matthews couldn't do that either and he was an outside right for twenty years. So Baxter must have done something right. Of course it's difficult to say if they could have won the European Cup before Celtic but Baxter's injury greatly stifled their ability to be creative in midfield and he was a loss. That '60s Rangers team were a very good side and the rest of Scottish football was infinitely stronger than it is now. Teams like Aberdeen, Hearts and the two Dundee sides took a bit of beating in those days. Rangers got to the final of the Cup Winners' Cup in 1967 but my feeling is they weren't good enough to win the European Cup. But, in saying that, six months before Celtic won in Lisbon, you would have said they weren't good enough to do it either. There was a huge surprise element when Celtic did it and paradoxically it was because Stein's team were thought not able to do it that they did it. Certain European sides didn't have their guard up against Celtic.

However, Rangers fan Hendry, despite being full of admiration for Stein's all-conquering Celtic side, is adamant the Ibrox men could have beaten them to the punch. He said: 'In 1964 we were approaching our peak and were capable of competing with the best in Europe. Celtic were a strong team in 1967 but they didn't have a ball player like Baxter in their team – he was inspirational. So yeah, there was a feeling of regret amongst the fans that they had done it before us. We had blown our chance two and a half years earlier.'

In season 1992/93, Walters Smith's side came within a goal of reaching the European Cup final in its revamped, Champions League format, the closest the Ibrox club have come to European success in recent years. Rangers fan William Sloan from Glasgow witnessed both Smith's and Symon's sides in action and the 80-year-old firmly believes the sixties team were the best Rangers have ever produced, even better than those before them which included legends like Willie Waddell, Bob McPhail and Willie Woodburn. He argues:

> I've seen so many great players at Ibrox but that team takes some beating. Baxter was undoubtedly the one who made them play. I'm not exaggerating to say that, along with Franz Beckenbauer, Slim Jim was up there with the best I've seen. Although they played in slightly different positions, Baxter had the class and gallusness of the German and he was a huge loss when he broke his leg. Rangers really struggled after that and the real tragedy is that he never got back to his best. As for Smith's team in the 90s – they were very good, with great team spirit but they didn't have the quality of a Baxter in the team.

Of course, in many ways, self-praise is no praise so let us consider the views of Brian Glanville, a respected London-based journalist and an expert on Italian football through his residence there in the 1960s. He is, of course, untainted by Old Firm influences. His brilliant book, *Champions of Europe* (about the history, romance and intrigue of the European Cup) contains the following thoughts in his chapter 'Milan and Inter' (pp 68–9): 'In the quarter-finals, Inter had emulated their rivals Milan by beating Glasgow Rangers, though they didn't win at Ibrox. Who knows what Rangers might have achieved had the wonderfully gifted left-half Jim Baxter not broken his leg helping Rangers beat Rapid in Vienna in the previous round.'

Still not convinced? Then what about Baxter actually proving he had the measure of Italian football months after his leg break, when he helped Scotland beat Italy at Hampden on 9 November 1965 in the World Cup qualifier at Hampden. The visitors that night contained four of the Inter team who played against Rangers over the two legs in February and March 1965. Sandro Mazzola was the attacking force common to both games but Aristide Guarneri (centre half), Giacinto Facchetti (left back) and Tarcisio Burgnich (right back) were the heart of Helenio Herrera's infamous *catenaccio* defence. However, not only did Baxter set up former Rangers teammate John Greig for the winning goal but he also found time to wind up his highly gifted opponents. Scots skipper Billy Bremner told the story of how the cocky number six spent the entire game nutmegging AC Milan's Gianni Rivera (the European Player of the Year in 1969 and inspiration for Milan's 1963 European Cup triumph) and then shouted over to the little ginger-haired midfielder, 'Hey, wee man – that's two . . . that's three'. Baxter, of course, was a Sunderland player by then but he could easily have been as influential a few months earlier as a Rangers player.

Football is full of ifs, buts and maybes but the argument concerning Baxter and Rangers' chances of winning the 1964/65 European Cup will carry on for ever and a day wherever Light Blues fans get together. There is no question that Baxter would have had an influence on the Rangers side over the two legs but it's impossible to say if they'd have beaten the Italians. It's also impossible to say if they would have then gone on to win the tournament .

You have to listen to someone like Eric Caldow, who maintains Baxter's control over Scot Symon's side was over-estimated and Crampsey who felt the Ibrox club were perhaps a little short in quality at that point. And when Gers fans like Robert Hendry and William Sloan claim a Baxter-inspired Rangers could have gone all the way that year, you accept that within such partisan views there is an element of wishful thinking.

On the other hand, when you hear respected figures in the

game like McNeill, Baillie and Glanville eulogising about Baxter's ability, and when you consider how well the big Fifer actually performed at the top level, then it would be foolish to dismiss the possibility that the famous trophy could and should have been captured by Rangers' 'Milan Maestros'.

4

A BLOT ON THE LANDSCAPE: THE SACKING OF SCOT SYMON

Chris Williamson

On 1 November 1967, the world was told that Scot Symon had been sacked as manager of Rangers Football Club. It was an episode in which the main protagonists, if alive today, would undoubtedly look back upon with a sense of great shame – not least because the Ibrox club were at that time top of the Scottish first division ahead of a Celtic side that had just won the European Cup.

The unassuming Gers boss had been in charge for just over thirteen years and had led the Govan men to six league championships, five Scottish Cup wins and four League Cup triumphs. During the treble season of 1963/64, Rangers chairman John Lawrence declared that Symon 'will be our manager for as long as he wants to stay', a bold proclamation even in an era when managers were seldom sacked on a whim.

As we know, football is a fickle business and the unspoken caveat is that Lawrence would have demanded that the success continued but there was no reason to believe that he was in any way dissatisfied with his manager at this stage. Three and a half years later, however, Lawrence had changed his tune completely. In a cowardly act he enlisted the help of a businessman to 'negotiate the terms' of Symon's resignation; a euphemism for the termination of the manager's contract. So, what had happened in the interim to necessitate such a course of action? Why had such a dedicated servant to Rangers, as Symon undoubtedly was, been treated in such an underhand manner? And was his replacement, Davie White, really the right man to be handed the reins at Ibrox?

James Scotland Symon was appointed manager of Rangers on 15 June 1954. He succeeded the legendary Bill Struth and, incredibly, was only the third boss in the Govan club's eighty-two-year history. It was the Perth-born man's second spell at Ibrox, having been signed as a player some sixteen years previously. Although he was to remain at the club, in the first instance, until 1947, Symon, officially, made only thirty-seven league appearances although he did contribute significantly to Rangers' wartime success, turning out on over 250 occasions and helping the club to ten trophies between 1939 and 1945.

After leaving Govan, Symon took over as manager of East Fife and, in a remarkable first season, guided the Methil club to League Cup success and the B division championship. This was not beginner's luck. The Fifers won the League Cup again in 1949, were runners-up in the 1950 Scottish Cup (to Rangers) and in five seasons in the top flight, Symon's side finished in third place twice and were fourth on another two occasions. Such feats did not go unnoticed and it was no surprise when the Scotsman was lured south of the border, to Preston North End, in March 1953. In his only full season in charge at Deepdale, North End finished eleventh in the old first division and reached the FA Cup final only to lose 3–2 to West Bromwich Albion. Symon, however, would not stay to improve upon these results; Bill Struth, now in his seventies, had decided that the time was right for him to stand down as Rangers manager and saw the Preston manager as his natural successor. It was an offer Symon could not refuse.

Following in Struth's footsteps was a daunting prospect. His association with the club went back four decades and during his thirty-four seasons as manager, Rangers were league champions eighteen times, Scottish Cup winners on ten occasions and League Cup winners twice, the latter competition having only been inaugurated in 1946. Added to this were eighteen Glasgow Cup and twenty Glasgow Charity Cup successes. Moreover, Struth had gained a reputation as the upholder and enforcer of a set of values that set Rangers apart from other football clubs. But, in Symon, the Ibrox legend was convinced he had found the ideal replacement. Announcing his successor's return to Ibrox, Struth stated:

> I came to know the qualities of Scot Symon when he joined us from Portsmouth. He was a man of indomitable courage, of unbreakable devotion to purpose, a man, indeed, who became a true Ranger, and no more imposing accolade could be given to anyone.

Symon's first season in charge, though, was a barren one with Rangers finishing third in the league and being eliminated from the League Cup and Scottish Cup at the quarter-final and sixth-round stages respectively. If he had been so inclined, the new manager could have used some valid excuses; players of the quality of Jock Shaw and Willie Thornton had decided to hang up their boots, while the likes of Bobby Brown, George Young, Sammy Cox and Willie Waddell were by now on the wrong side of thirty. The *sine die* suspension of defender Willie Woodburn a week and a half into the 1954/55 campaign did little to help matters.

Therefore, it was to Symon's enormous credit that Rangers won league championships in 1956, 1957 and 1959 during what was essentially a period of transition for the club. The second half of the decade saw a number of players arrive at Ibrox who were to make significant short- and long-term contributions to the club. Don Kichenbrand, a burly South African striker from Delfos, fell into the former category, propelling Rangers to the title with twenty-four league goals during the 1955/56 season, while the likes of Jimmy Millar, Bobby Shearer, Harold Davis and Ian McMillan served with distinction for many years. The signing of Jim Baxter of Raith Rovers in June 1960 was seen as the final piece in what would be a colourful jigsaw.

Symon's managerial philosophy was relatively simple – put the best players in their favoured position and let them get on with it. Thankfully, his players obliged and with Baxter and McMillan creating, Alex Scott and Davie Wilson providing and scoring from the wings, and Millar and Ralph Brand up front, Rangers were a potent attacking force. The league and League Cup double was completed in 1960/61 and, that same season, the Light Blues became the first Scottish team to reach a European final, only to be defeated 4–1 on aggregate by Fiorentina in the Cup Winners' Cup. Rangers won both domestic cup competitions in 1961/62, but were runners-up to Dundee in the league. John Greig, Ronnie McKinnon and Willie Henderson all made their breakthroughs during this season and each would go on to give over a decade of outstanding service to the club.

By the end of 1962/63, a season in which Rangers won the league and Scottish Cup, a team considered by many observers as the best ever to represent the club had fallen into place. This renowned starting eleven consisted of Ritchie, Shearer, Caldow, Greig, McKinnon, Baxter, Henderson, McMillan, Millar, Brand and Wilson and combined, according to club historian David Mason, to give: 'youth and experience, strength and subtlety'. Domestically they were unstoppable, achieving a clean sweep of trophies in 1963/64. The League Cup was in the cabinet by the end of October, after a 5–0 win over Morton in the final, while Dundee lost out to Rangers in both the league race and Scottish Cup final. However, the superstars of Real Madrid put an end to any European Cup dreams the club may have had, demolishing the Ibrox side 7–0 on aggregate in the preliminary round. Despite this setback John Lawrence voiced his unequivocal support for Symon. The next season a League Cup final win over Celtic only slightly tempered the disappointment of a final league placing of fifth and a third round Scottish Cup exit at the hands of Hibernian. However, ominously for Rangers, on the Monday following the cup victory over Symon's men, the Edinburgh club's manager, Jock Stein, left to take over at Celtic.

Between the end of the second world war and 1965, the Parkhead side had been in the doldrums. While Rangers were picking up silverware on a regular basis, Celtic had drifted off the radar completely. Only twice did they finish above their Glasgow rivals, and they had won only one league championship out of a possible nineteen. The main challengers to Rangers during this time were Hibs and Hearts and, to a lesser extent, Aberdeen, Dundee and Kilmarnock. But Stein's arrival reinvigorated the Parkhead club to a degree not even the most fervent Hoops fan would have imagined possible.

Stein had played for Celtic as a defender during the 1950s and took over youth coaching duties at the club following his retirement through injury. The Burnbank man's first managerial role, however, came at Dunfermline following his appointment in April 1960. The Pars were in a perilous position, needing to win their final half dozen games in order to avoid relegation. No-one would have blamed Stein if they had dropped out of the top flight but, amazingly, he guided them to the required six consecutive victories and to safety. The Fifers never looked back, winning the Scottish Cup the following year and taking part in European competition in all-bar two seasons during the 1960s. Stein left East End Park at the end of the 1963/64 campaign to take over at Hibs and, while fans of the Leith club would no doubt have cursed the brevity of his stay at Easter Road, they could at least be thankful for his leaving them in relatively good health.

Rangers' disposition, however, was soon to be a cause for concern. Football was entering a new era and Stein and Symon's managerial styles were at polar extremes. According to Sandy Jardine, the Gers manager was not always a visible presence at Ibrox:

> Scot Symon was old-school, having come up under Bill Struth. Everybody had a lot of respect for Symon but you only saw him on a Tuesday and a Thursday and then again on match day. That was because, in those days, the manager had a huge amount of administration duties and he was more office bound as opposed to being on the training pitch. But football started to change in the mid-60s; it became more tactical, more about preparation and more about spending time with the players.

Jardine's sentiments are echoed by former Rangers and Scotland defender Eric Caldow who, in an interview for *The Rangers Historian* in 1987, claimed Symon was, 'set in his ways,' and was, 'not a tactical man'. He continued: 'Scot Symon didn't talk to you about your immediate opponent. He had the attitude that we should let the opposition worry about us.'

By contrast, Stein was one of the new breed of tracksuit managers; those who would conduct training themselves and who would react to situations tactically as and when required when games were in progress. Perhaps more importantly, Stein refused to accept any meaningful input from the Parkhead board. Symon, apparently, had no such luxury.

Stein could do little to stop Celtic finishing in an abysmal eighth place in 1964/65 season although he did at least give the Parkhead fans their first taste of success for eight years when they beat Dunfermline 3–2 in the Scottish Cup final. The fact that he felt the need to release no fewer than twenty-five players at the end of that season illustrated that he had little confidence in the squad he had inherited. The Parkhead board, if they were to live up to their reputation for parsimony, were unlikely to throw money at the problem. It was therefore necessary for Stein to begin putting faith in some of those youngsters he had worked with previously in his time as a coach at Celtic Park. And so emerged players of the calibre of Bobby Murdoch, Steve Chalmers, Bobby Lennox and Jimmy Johnstone; players who would form the backbone of the Lisbon Lions.

Over on the blue side of the city, the talismanic but troubled playmaker Jim Baxter's leg break earlier that season against Rapid Vienna had ended the Ibrox club's genuine European Cup aspirations. As it turned out, it was the beginning of the end for the Fifer and, when fit again, he made the journey south of the border in May 1965; Sunderland being the destination.

Baxter's departure was obviously a great loss to the club; he was arguably the most skilful player ever to pull on the light-blue jersey. But with the acquisition of Danish pair Jorn Sorenson and Kai Johansen from Morton, and the continued development of cousins Alec Willoughby and Jim Forrest, there was good reason to be optimistic that Rangers could wrest back the championship trophy in 1965/66.

Symon's men drew first blood, taking both points from the Ibrox Old Firm match in September thanks to goals from Forrest and George McLean. Celtic gained revenge at New Year, however, coming from behind and scoring all their goals in the second half to record a 5–1 victory on a frosty Parkhead pitch. The defeat did not appear to have any lasting effect on Rangers, though, as they won their next five league games, scoring fifteen goals in the process. But a dreadful series of results in March when they lost to Falkirk and Dundee United, and could manage only draws with Hearts and Kilmarnock, severely dented their title aspirations and allowed Celtic to claim their first league championship in eleven years. The Parkhead side had overcome Rangers in October's League Cup final, so when the sides met once more in the Scottish Cup final at the end of the season, the pressure was on Symon's men to prevent their rivals from completing a domestic treble. The rejuvenated Celts went into the game as favourites but Kai Johansen's famous goal in the replay (after the first match was drawn 0–0) ensured that the cup headed back to Ibrox. But, in reality, the pendulum had swung towards the East End and it would stay there for the next decade.

Celtic's defence of their newly acquired title got off to a good start in season 1966/67, with seven wins from seven games including a 2–0 home victory over Rangers in September. And after another defeat at the hands of their rivals, in October's League Cup final (by 1–0), the pressure began to mount on Symon. This was uncharted territory for the Ibrox club and there were suggestions that Rangers should start to look for a manager capable of beating Stein at his own game. Bizarre rumours that Real Madrid legend Ferenc Puskas was being lined up for a coaching job at Ibrox came to nothing but a concrete offer was made to Aberdeen's Eddie Turnbull at the beginning of November. Had he accepted, Turnbull would have become Symon's assistant and would likely have succeeded him as manager. As it was, he declined, later revealing that it was a decision he greatly regretted. Just over a fortnight after the approach to Turnbull, Dundee's Bobby Seith was appointed as coach.

Despite the injection of fresh ideas, Rangers found themselves four points behind their rivals at Christmas. However, not long into the New Year, the talk was not of the league championship race but of the Scottish Cup and the most embarrassing scoreline the Govan club have ever been on the end of; Berwick Rangers 1, Rangers 0.

The infamous match took place at Shielfield Park on 27 January 1967, a date that all Rangers fans have tried to bury in the darkest recesses of their minds. Sammy Reid, a self-confessed bluenose, scored the all-important goal and ended Rangers' defence of the trophy at the first hurdle. The gravity of the situation was not lost on Symon. As the Ibrox players sat in the dressing room stunned and trying to come to terms with the enormity of their defeat, it was their shocked boss who apparently broke the silence by muttering: 'There will be hell to pay for this. This is terrible. There will be hell to pay for this.'

Symon must have feared for his own job after what he admitted was, 'the worst result in the club's history,' but he received public backing from his chairman. 'There is no doubt in my mind,' John Lawrence raged, 'that the only people who can be blamed for this defeat are the ones on the field – the players!' He was in unforgiving mood and stated that the 'humiliating result' would be high on the agenda at the next board meeting.

Perhaps that result should in itself have signalled the end for Symon. Celtic manager John Barnes would have no such stay of execution when he led the Parkhead side to their devastating 3–1 Scottish Cup defeat to Inverness almost forty years later. The former Liverpool player was literally on his way out before the fans could properly gather their thoughts and show their discontent. But this was a different era and Symon lived to fight another day. It was two of his players who were made scapegoats.

George McLean and Jim Forrest never kicked a ball (in a competitive match at least) for Rangers again and there is no doubt that this knee-jerk decision hindered the club both in the short and the long term. The treatment of both players, Forrest in particular, was incredibly harsh. Their goal-scoring records at Rangers were highly commendable; McLean had netted 82 times in 117 games, while Forrest's 145 goals in 164 appearances was nothing short of sensational. The latter was a mere twenty-two years of age at the time and as David Mason reflected:

Here was a youngster singled out among a team of seasoned internationals for his failure to find the net in one 90-minute spell of play. . . . There is little doubt that he could have served Rangers well for many years, having benefited from the experience of Berwick, but it was not to be.

Forrest asked to be placed on the transfer list on 7 February and the next month signed for Preston North End for a fee of £38,000. McLean followed him out of Ibrox three weeks later when he moved to Dundee in exchange for Andy Penman and £30,000.

In an interview in 2002, as part of the build up to Rangers' return to Berwick for a Scottish Cup tie, Forrest spoke of his hurt at being blamed for the awful result on that fateful day at Shielfield and for not being recognised for the many significant contributions he made to Rangers. Poignantly, he pointed out that, 'as a team we won together, and as a team we should all have taken equal responsibility when we lost'. Forrest, not surprisingly, was also disappointed by his manager's reaction to him in the aftermath of the cup tie. 'I was never given the opportunity to sit down and talk with the manager, or any of the directors, as to why I was being booted out,' he claimed. 'I still feel to this day that Symon owed me an explanation but he took the coward's way out and he simply wouldn't discuss it with me and before I knew it I was gone.'

George McLean, who during his spell at Ibrox was seen as something of a Jack the Lad character, was rather more pragmatic. 'I would loved to have stayed on to play at Ibrox, but it didn't work out that way,' he told *The Scotsman* in 2002. 'There is no point in looking back. At every team I went to after that I finished top goalscorer, so life went on.'

It is generally accepted that the decision to jettison Forrest and McLean was not Symon's alone. The Rangers boss was probably pressurised into this course of action by the board of directors. However, as David Mason points out, 'even if this were the case, Symon could have made a stand if he felt there was an injustice. The fact that he didn't . . . suggests that he was at least party to the decision. It was one that would haunt him to the end of his days at Ibrox.'

Rangers tried to get on with their league challenge as best they could. Alec Willoughby made his first start of the season on 4 February, at home to Hearts, and notched a hat-trick in a 5–1 win, a game that marked the debuts of both Sandy Jardine and Colin Jackson. Willoughby went on to score an incredible sixteen goals in eleven games but a 1–0 home defeat at the hands of Dunfermline on April Fool's day, together with draws against Clyde and Dundee later that month, proved costly.

Celtic went to Ibrox on 6 May and left with the point they needed to secure the championship for the second consecutive season. Amazingly, and significantly, it was the Parkhead club's first back-to-back titles for half a century. A week earlier they had beaten Aberdeen at Hampden to win the Scottish Cup and, to the dismay of Rangers fans, the Bhoys then went on to claim the biggest prize of them all, the European Cup, by defeating Inter Milan in the final on 25 May 1967.

Almost bizarrely, Rangers and Symon still had a chance to salvage some pride and make history of their own just one week later. Having overcome Glentoran, Borussia Dortmund, Real Zaragoza (albeit on the toss of a coin) and Slavia Sofia in the previous rounds, Symon's men embarked on their journey to Nuremberg where they would do battle with a talented Bayern Munich side on 31 May in the Cup Winners' Cup final. Returning with the trophy would have been a major achievement given that it was more or less a home game for the Bavarians. But, having reached the end of a season to forget, the pressure to succeed was now enormous.

Unfortunately, chairman John Lawrence's curious pre-match comments did little to help team morale. On the eve of the final he, 'publicly condemned the players and Symon, sacked the chief scout and proclaimed that Celtic were the yardstick against which Rangers' achievements had to be measured.' Symon then made what turned out to be a career-defining mistake by opting to start the game with the considerable physical presence of Roger Hynd in the centre-forward berth, a decision akin to Alex McLeish starting with Marvin Andrews in attack. Hynd was big and strong but, alas, never a player of the highest quality; by his own admission he was 'of limited ability'. Nevertheless, he had played as an emergency centre-for-ward in a reserve match towards the end of the same season and scored four goals.

On the back of this aberration, Symon promoted him to the starting eleven at the expense of the in-form Willoughby for the second leg of the semi-final against Slavia Sofia. Despite looking out of his depth, Hynd kept his place in the team for the Gers' final league match of the season against Celtic and rewarded his man-ager's faith with an equaliser nine minutes from time. His selection for the match in Germany, however, still baffled many Rangers fans. How could a player who was a defender by trade and who had only played a handful of top-level matches in the centre-forward position, begin the match ahead of a young out-and-out goalscorer whose form had been electrifying? Willoughby was as disillusioned as the fans and asked for a transfer. Of course, had the gamble worked, the fans would not have questioned Symon's judgement. But, as it transpired, this controversial decision was the major talking point of the Nuremberg post-mortem.

The best chance of the game, as fate would have it, fell to Hynd just after the half-hour mark. Alas, when presented with it six yards from goal after good work from Dave Smith, the big man fluffed his lines, knocking the ball weakly into the arms of Munich's German international goalkeeper Sepp Maier when it seemed easier to score. Franz Roth struck for the Germans with just eleven minutes to go in extra time and there was no way back for Rangers.

David Mason recalled the mood following the dejected Govan side's arrival back in Scotland:

When the team returned to Glasgow they faced an Ibrox support that was completely disenchanted and crestfallen. Celebrations at the other side of the city, meanwhile, pro-claimed Celtic as champions of Europe. While Rangers and Symon should have received credit for reaching a European final for the second time, they faced only condemnation for failure. In reality, Celtic's victory over Inter Milan at Lisbon had already undermined that achievement before a ball was kicked in Nuremberg.

Symon must have felt the Sword of Damocles hanging over his head and, arguably, that was the second opportunity after Berwick for the Ibrox board to make the change. While the Rangers boss had escaped the worst of the criticism after the Scottish Cup exit, his chairman now seemed less supportive and there were also dissenting voices amongst the playing squad. Some of this criticism was warranted. Had Forrest and McLean been allowed to continue their Ibrox careers Rangers might have won in Nuremberg, and indeed may have gone into that game as Scottish champions.

As it was, Rangers were reeling during the summer of 1967. Symon had a massive task on his hands to lift his troops and prepare them for the following campaign and, to help him, Davie White had been drafted in. White had been successful during a fifteen-month spell in charge of Clyde and was brought to the club with the long-term prospect of succeeding Symon, although the club publicly denied this at the time. The new man had shown a desire to learn and broaden his coaching horizons by shadowing both Stein and Symon on their respective European-final excursions and it was during the trip to Germany that he was asked by the Rangers manager to join the staff at Ibrox.

Whatever misgivings the Rangers board now had about Symon, they backed their manager financially. Striker Alex Ferguson was secured from Dunfermline for a Scottish record transfer fee of £65,000, along with keeper Eric Sorensen and winger Orjan Persson, with Davie Wilson and Jimmy Millar departing. An early test of Rangers' appetite for the test which lay ahead was afforded to Symon in the League Cup sectional phase, which saw the Ibrox side grouped with Aberdeen, Dundee United and Celtic. The hapless Light Blues, however, would miss crucial penalties in both ties against their Old Firm rivals and exit the competition at the first hurdle. This failure against the Parkhead men was arguably the beginning of the end for Symon, despite the Govan men's quick response.

Rangers managed to recover from this disappointment. In their opening eight league games of season 1967/68, the Ibrox men won six – including a 1–0 home victory over Celtic – and drew two to leave them top of the table. After escaping from the brutality of Berwick and the horror of Hynd, Symon seemed to have weathered another storm although the fans were still far from happy and the directors less than publicly supportive. Nevertheless, it was still a shock when it was announced on 1 November 1967 that his reign as manager of Rangers had come to an end.

It was the cowardly manner in which Symon was dismissed that lent the gentlemanly Ibrox boss enduring sympathy. A board meeting convened on the evening of 31 October and it was agreed that the time had come to bring down the curtain on their manager's career. However, rather than inform Symon himself, Lawrence shamefully instructed Alex McBain, an accountant with no formal connection to the club, to deliver the news. The Gers boss was summoned to McBain's home and, in his own words, 'was informed that . . . it was decided to terminate my appointment as manager forthwith. I was stunned – that was the only way to describe it.'

The news, when it broke the next morning, sent shockwaves through Scottish football. A club that purported to embody the traditional Scottish virtues of loyalty, fairness and dignity had acted with heartless insensitivity. Bobby Seith was dismayed and resigned immediately. 'I no longer want to be part of an organisation which can treat a loyal servant so badly,' he blasted. Seith stayed long enough to persuade the raging Alex Ferguson not to follow him out of the door. In his autobiography, *Alex Ferguson: Managing my Life*, the legendary Manchester United boss recalled how that period:

. . . made me sick at the treatment inflicted on the manager. I was shocked, disillusioned and in a way frightened. How could Rangers Football Club do this, with a team undefeated in the league and sitting at the top of the table. . . . How could a club of great tradition be capable of such behaviour?

Sandy Jardine, looking back on the episode some twenty-seven year later, recalled the players' mood upon hearing the news: 'Even though the defeat to Berwick earlier in the year had been a huge shock,' he said, 'everyone was absolutely gobsmacked because we were top of the league at the time.' The manner of the dismissal was also called into question. 'It wasn't handled properly,' Jardine added: 'For someone who had given the service and had the success that he had, it should have been handled a lot, lot better. It basically shattered Scot and he didn't come back to the club until he returned as manager of Partick Thistle some eight years' later.'

A backtracking Lawrence claimed that, rather than being sacked, Symon had actually resigned after turning down a new contract. In a further attempt to justify the decision the chairman said: 'The goals were not forthcoming even though we spent a lot of money on players on Mr Symon's advice. This position just could not continue indefinitely.' Lawrence apparently saw no irony in his part in the decision to get rid of Forrest and McLean the previous season.

The chairman did not look far for Symon's replacement, as Davie White, sooner than anticipated, made the step up to the hot seat. But was the former Clyde manager the man to tackle Stein? Alex Ferguson remembers that the new Rangers manager had, 'looked a bit perplexed' and labelled him 'ineffective'. White saw no need radically to alter the team's playing style; he had, after all, inherited a team that was unbeaten and top of the league, even if they weren't scoring as many goals as the chairman wanted. Rangers won nine league games on the trot prior to the season's fourth Old

Firm clash on 2 January 1968 that would be, as usual, the acid test. Twice the Ibrox men fell behind but twice they battled back and Johansen was again the hero, scoring the second equaliser with two minutes remaining.

Rangers went on to rack up another nine consecutive league wins but in April they dropped vital points on the road, drawing away at both Dundee United and Morton. It was just the slip-up Celtic were waiting for and they overtook the Gers on the home straight to record their third league title in a row.

It says something for the quality of Stein's side that Rangers lost only one league game all season, and that on the last day, and still finished second. There was no luck in the cup competitions either: after a 0–0 draw at Ibrox, Leeds triumphed 2–0 at Elland Road to send Rangers out of the Fairs Cup at the quarter-final stage; while Hearts got the better of White's troops after a third round Scottish Cup replay. The trophy cabinet would remain empty.

It was a similar story in season 1968/69. Having lost twice to Jock Stein's side in the League Cup again, Rangers got the better of Celtic in their league encounters, winning 4–2 at Parkhead in September and 1–0 at Ibrox in the New Year match. White had paid a Scottish record £100,000 to Hibs for Colin Stein at the end of October 1968, and followed this up with the £50,000 purchase of Alex MacDonald from St Johnstone three weeks' later. Stein made an immediate impact, scoring two hat-tricks and a brace in his first three matches, but his temperament was suspect and he was sent off against both Kilmarnock and Clyde. He was suspended for seven of the final eight league games, during which time Rangers threw away points against Airdrie, Dundee United, Aberdeen and Dundee (on two occasions). The telling statistic is that Rangers dropped eight points during this spell, and lost the title to Celtic by five. The Gers' misery was compounded by a 4–0 humiliation at the hands of their Glasgow rivals in the Scottish Cup final. It was little consolation that Rangers performed well in Europe again, reaching the semi-final of the Fairs Cities Cup (the 1960s equivalent of the UEFA Cup) where they were eliminated by Newcastle United, the eventual winners.

Celtic's continued success, and White's inability to put a stop to it, rankled with both the Ibrox support and those with influence in the boardroom. Jim Baxter was re-signed during the close season and he inspired Rangers to a League Cup win over the champions at home in August. However, a howler from goalkeeper Gerry Neef a week later gifted Tommy Gemmell a winning goal at Parkhead, and for the third year in a row Celtic progressed from the group at Rangers' expense. An indifferent start to the league campaign saw the Govan men occupy sixth place after eleven games, although they were only two points behind leaders Dundee United. The Gers boss was under pressure from the supporters and the press, with Ibrox legend Willie Waddell – in his role as a journalist – the most scathing critic. The fact that Waddell would ultimately get his wish and succeed White was not unrelated. Two far from impressive perform-ances in the second round of the Cup Winners' Cup, which saw Rangers beaten 3–1 both home and away by Gornik Zabrze, sealed White's fate. After the second leg at Ibrox, a number of fans gath-ered on Edmiston Drive to call for the manager's head. The next morning White was dismissed.

Nevertheless, many observers are of the opinion that Davie White was unlucky to have been in charge of Rangers at a time when Jock Stein's Celtic ruled the roost. 'Most people agree with the theory that the job came too soon for him,' said veteran sports journalist Rodger Baillie, before adding that, 'White's spell at Rangers is at best a footnote in Rangers history. The sad thing is, he was, in fact, not a bad manager and had demonstrated that during his successful spell with Clyde.'

Sandy Jardine concurred with this view:

Davie White was a modern manager, but he was maybe

thrown in just too early. If he had another couple of years to get his feet under the table, then it could have all so different. But his biggest problem of the lot was the Celtic team of that time. It was the greatest team in their history, led by one of the greatest managers in Scottish football. But Davie was an astute manager and he proved that after he left Rangers when he had a successful spell at Dundee.

White himself, although reluctant to elaborate on his time at Ibrox, acknowledged, 'You have to win one of the major honours for this club before the fans and the people in football think of you as successful.'

Celtic's renaissance, and subsequent dominance, under Stein had come as a surprise to the Ibrox club, and an unwelcome one at that. In what was to become, post-1965, a two-horse race for the Scottish championship, a second-place finish was tantamount to abject failure. Symon and White both failed to keep pace with the Parkhead side and paid the price. Indeed, their dismissals can be seen as marking the beginning of a trend in which one Old Firm manager pays for the successes of the other. This has recently been illustrated in cases such as Tommy Burns, John Barnes, Lou Macari and Dick Advocaat.

However, there are ways and means to deal with failure. During a press conference in May 2005, the current Rangers manager, Alex McLeish, launched a thinly veiled attack on Celtic and Hearts (both of whom had questioned the integrity of match officials during the 2004/05 season) by stating that, 'the institution that is Rangers has been unsurpassed in 132 years in terms of dignity'. Although McLeish's arithmetic was derived from the club's official birth date of 1873, it is difficult to disagree with such a statement. Through the years the club has faced up to defeat with grace, where others have chosen to wallow in paranoia and lay blame at the door of anyone but themselves. Indeed, we often hear of the 'Rangers way', whereby those associated with the club have either closed ranks under a barrage of criticism or have refused personally to profit from dishing the dirt on their time at Ibrox.

However, the sacking of Scot Symon is certainly a blot on that particular landscape. The former Rangers boss gave over two decades of his life to the club, conducting himself throughout in a manner that would have made his mentor, Bill Struth, incredibly proud. Yet his chairman John Lawrence could not bring himself to inform Symon, man to man, of the board's decision to relieve him of his duties. And he compounded his cowardice by refusing to be honest about the sacking.

Rangers probably needed to make a change to compete with the managerial phenomenon that was Jock Stein. The hasty appointment of White was the wrong decision and, although a costly mistake, it would be rectified in time. But the nasty taste that was left by the sacking of James Scotland Symon will linger for many years to come.

5

DEATH ON STAIRWAY 13

Graham Walker

In immediate, swift reaction, Danny turned then and, without a word to his neighbours, started to fight his way to the top of the terracing and along the fence that crowned it to the stairs and the open gate. To the feelings of those he jostled and pushed he gave not the slightest thought. Now the battle was for a place in the Subway, and he ran as soon as he could, hurtling down the road, into the odorous maw of Copland Road station and through the closing door of a train that had already started on its journey northwards.

(George Blake, *The Shipbuilders*)

The novelist George Blake's description of fans exiting the east terracing at Ibrox stadium after a Rangers–Celtic game was published in 1935. The book's central character, Danny, a riveter in the Clydeside shipyards, has just joyfully greeted the final whistle and a satisfying result for his Rangers heroes. It is the culmination of the fictional portrayal of an afternoon of typically passionate involvement amidst a massive crowd of similarly fanatical working men.

A generation later, at the beginning of 1971, Blake's evocative passages took on an eerie prescience. For, on 2 January, following another Old Firm clash at Ibrox, crowd pressure on one of the huge east terrace's exits – stairway 13, the nearest to the subway station – resulted in the deaths of 66 fans and injuries to a further 145. As in the 1930s the crowd – over 80,000 strong – was overwhelmingly composed of male manual workers like the young Danny. To complete the symmetry, the fans departed the terracing in a state of elation occasioned by a Rangers goal with virtually the match's last kick.

The disaster was the worst involving sports spectators that the British Isles had known until that date. In terms of the death toll it surpassed the previous major football-match tragedies of Bolton, in 1946, and Ibrox again back in 1902. The latter case – which occurred during a Scotland–England international – was the result of the collapse of a section of the west terracing. It resembled the 1971 case in respect of the crucial factor of crowd pressure: the nature of spectating at major football matches in Britain changed little from the beginning of the twentieth century to the years nearing its close. Crushing was common and fans often lost control of their movements while watching the game and leaving the ground afterwards.

Following Ibrox in 1971, crowd-safety issues began to be addressed more purposefully and new legislation was introduced. Rangers embarked upon the radical reconstruction of Ibrox into a predominantly seated stadium by 1981, and an all-seater by the mid-1990s. However, it was only after the Hillsborough disaster of 1989 – which eclipsed 1971 in loss of life – that the general character of crowd culture in British football changed.

Rangers fans had little reason for optimism going to the 2 January game. I, then a 14-year-old schoolboy, recall the sense of dread which accompanied contemplation of defeat, the knowledge that Rangers' championship hopes would be extinguished and those of Celtic, particularly in relation to then challengers Aberdeen, greatly enhanced. The hopes of bluenoses rested heavily with the Dons, a capable side that included former Ibrox stars (and cousins) Jim Forrest and Alex Willoughby. Between them they had provided

James Bowie (second from left) in a Rangers team photo from 1921. To Bowie's right, at the end of the row, is the great Alan Morton. However, the *Wee Blue Devil's* presence on the Rangers board in June 1947 could not save Bowie from being ousted as chairman. (courtesy Mirrorpix)

WILLIE WOODBURN (RANGERS) - CENTRE HALF

Willie Woodburn, one of the greatest Scottish centre backs of all time.
But his *sine die* suspension by the SFA in 1954 sent shockwaves
through the game. (courtesy Mirrorpix)

The one and only Jim Baxter, in typical pose, after engineering yet another triumph at Celtic's expense in 1963. Many Rangers fans felt that his leg break against Rapid Vienna in 1964 cost the club the European Cup. (courtesy Mirrorpix)

Rangers manager Scot Symon, with one of his many excellent sides, in September 1961. Back row: Bobby Shearer, Eric Caldow, Billy Ritchie, Harold Davis, Bill Paterson, Jim Baxter. Front row, Symon, Alex Scott, Ian McMillan, Jimmy Millar, Ralph Brand, Davie Wilson. (courtesy Empics)

OFFICIAL PROGRAMME

RANGERS

The excitement of the packed Hampden terracing creates an atmosphere you find nowhere else in the world.

v.

SCOTTISH
LEAGUE
CUP FINAL

MORTON

PRICE
6ᴰ.

Kick-off
3 p.m.

SATURDAY, 26th OCTOBER 1963
HAMPDEN PARK · GLASGOW

OFFICIAL PROGRAMME

Scottish

1ˢ

CUP FINAL

RANGERS (HOLDERS) v CELTIC
HAMPDEN PARK, MAY 4, 1963

KICK-OFF
3 P.M.

Programmes featuring two of the trophies won by Scot Symon at Ibrox: the Scottish Cup of May, 1963 and the League Cup of October, 1963. Sir Alex Ferguson said that Symon's sacking, 'made me sick at the treatment of the manager'.

The battle of Hampden. The consequences of Old Firm fans fighting after the 1980 Scottish Cup final were far-reaching for the clubs and Scottish football. (courtesy SMG)

The arrival of Graeme Souness at Ibrox as player-manager in April 1986 revolutionised Rangers and Scottish football.

Three years later, Souness broke with tradition and signed Mo Johnston (seen here playing for Rangers against Dundee United in 1990) from under the noses of Celtic.

Tore Andre Flo (on the right, with Shota Arveladze, left) was
bought from Chelsea for £12.5 million in 2000. The Scottish-record
signing epitomised the high-spending Dick Advocaat era.
(courtesy Mirrorpix)

my earliest and most cherished football memory: a 5–0 League Cup final triumph over Morton in season 1963/64 that I had cheered from one of Hampden Park's famous slopes, the old lady of a stadium accommodating well over 100,000 on the day.

I went to Ibrox ticketless, more in hope of securing one than expectation. I stood on the Copland Road for an hour before the match started, pleading in vain for a 'spare' while the crowd surged up the road singing lustily. 'Who put the ball in the Celtic net? Derek! Derek!' in honour of a precocious Derek Johnstone's headed winner in the League Cup final a couple of months before. However, the team had slumped since that day, and it looked like that glorious result would merely interrupt the depressing sequence of Celtic victories.

Like many others I waited outside the ground after the match started, resigned to judging the progress of the game by the roars, until the gates were opened not long after the start of the second half. This was standard practice in Scotland then and, as a boy, I took advantage of it many times at Ibrox, and especially at Hampden, to catch the later stages of cup finals and internationals. Sometimes – and 2 January 1971 would be another example – this would be the part of the match most packed with drama. A witness at the Fatal Accident Inquiry (FAI) after the Ibrox disaster – a resident of the tenement building opposite stairway 13 – referred to the practice as 'the Aberdeen gate'. By this he meant that the fans who gained access to the ground in this way got in for nothing, his remark thus grounded in the popular (among Glaswegians) stereotype of Aberdonians as tight-fisted. Amidst the official police evidence is the testimony of Peter Semple, a 31-year-old journalist with the *Sunday Mail* and then on strike, who went to the match as a spectator and entered the ground at 4.05 p.m., ten minutes into the second half. Semple's story forms part of the fascinating, if factually flawed, account of the disaster by fellow journalist John Burrowes in his book, *Frontline Report*.

When the gates opened I, along with many others like Semple, galloped up the steps of stairway 13. Due to the density of the crowd at the north-east corner I made my way along the back of the terracing to the stand side and worked my way down till I got a reasonable view. As the game – goalless – apparently petered to a close the Rangers end suddenly burst out with a rendition of 'The Northern Lights of Old Aberdeen' in support of the title-chasers. In its melodious and folksy way it formed a surreal contrast to the usual acerbic terracing anthems, and possibly also carried the influence of the then customary Hogmanay sing-song. Then, out of nothing, a long-range shot from Celtic's Lennox struck the crossbar in front of me. The ball looped up in the air and fell to the smallest player on the pitch, Jimmy Johnstone, to nod into the net. Despondency instantly enveloped the east terracing and some fans turned for the exits before the match was restarted. There was only a minute left to play. I recall an insensate fan turning and headbutting a fellow bluenose for no apparent reason other than his own frustration. I watched despairingly through the haze of freezing fog that had crept over the stadium as Rangers launched a last attack. A free kick was won on the left and the ball dispatched into the penalty box where, amidst a ruck of players, Colin Stein, the Rangers centre forward, lashed home the equaliser. The goal was so gloriously unexpected: it was a period in which Rangers fans were prone to fatalism where Old Firm games and twists of fortune were concerned. It now seemed that we had defied the fates and as a consequence the relief and the joy were overwhelming. I have never been part of such an intense goal celebration, even when the goals were match and trophy winners. In the FAI the chief superintendent of police described the scenes of delirium: 'The excitement was tremendous, jubilation, they were singing, shouting, they were jumping up and down, waving their arms, hugging their friends, the terracing was in an uproar. I would say it was football mania at its highest.' The Rangers chairman, John Lawrence, later expressed the view that the fans' euphoric state had much to do with what happened on stairway 13. An eyewitness who lived opposite claimed that the Rangers goal instilled such 'energy and exuberance' among the fans that due care was not taken on the stairway.

Indeed, I recall that the wild celebrations continued among the fans with whom I exited from the south-east steps of the terracing (the alternative exit to stairway 13 from the east terracing) some seven to eight minutes after the end of the match. I departed blithely unaware of the tragedy unfolding yards away, and it was only as I waited for a train about half an hour later that the first word of it was conveyed to me by fellow supporters who had heard radio reports. Shortly after arriving home my father, on the backshift at his work on the *Daily Record*, phoned to check that I was safe and told me of the enormity of the events. My mother and I then turned to the news and began the grim business of trying to comprehend what had occurred. On that night, and on many subsequent occasions, I had cause to consider myself extremely fortunate: the exit I took from the ground in those days depended entirely on proximity to where I had stood watching the match. I had used stairway 13 probably as much as any other exit in the past.

In the days following the disaster a theory was floated as to its cause, which quickly took root, and has persisted in accounts of the event to the present. It was suggested that many Rangers fans in the course of departing down stairway 13 after Celtic's goal heard the roar which greeted Stein's equaliser, and attempted to return by climbing back up the steps. In so doing, the theory ran, they collided with fans leaving when the match ended, thus causing a deadly crush. The widespread currency enjoyed by this explanation led Colin Stein to admit twenty years' later to the anguish he felt about possibly, if of course unwittingly, being responsible for the accident. The theory has endured in spite of the absence of evidence to support it in the findings of the FAI, and of the efforts of fans – many of whom were at the match and witnessed what happened – to explode it.

The evidence of the proceedings at the FAI, and a subsequent court case taken by the relatives of one of the victims against Rangers, reveals the much more probable cause to have been that of someone stumbling and falling almost halfway down the staircase, precipitating a surge forward by the densely-packed crowd. Bodies, the police evidence stated, were piled on bodies to a height of some six feet, and the victims, some of whom died standing, had the life literally sucked from them. The cause of death for the vast majority was traumatic asphyxiation. It was also made clear that the fatal accident occurred some minutes after the end of the match – the most common estimate was between four and five although some were inclined to put it later. The match ended at 16.41, and chief inspector Marshall Pretswell gave evidence that he was informed at 16.50 by a spectator who had come back down the terracing to the trackside that there had been an accident. The first call for an ambulance was made at 16.53. Other police evidence states that the first emergency call came at 16.47, but adds that there is reason to believe that this time was incorrectly logged.

In the minds of all witnesses bar one – who testified to seeing a single individual attempting to go back up the stairway – there was no question of fans coming down colliding with fans going up. Several witnesses claim to have seen, or been aware of, someone falling in front of them as they descended the stairs, and there were those eyewitnesses, both on the stairway and watching from the tenement flats opposite the exit, who laid great stress on the possibility that someone on top of a friend's shoulders in a posture of celebration lost balance, toppled and created a snowball effect. The conclusion of the FAI was that the precise cause remained obscure but that the effective cause was the overwhelming crowd pressure on the stairway.

The perils of large crowds using exits at football stadia were well recognised, but Ibrox had an especially ominous recent history. In 1961 – again following an Old Firm game in which Rangers scored a late equaliser – two fans were killed in an accident on the same stairway. At this time the steep exit was divided only by a wooden handrail down the middle, which gave way in the crush. Fans were able to escape to the grass banking alongside the stairway by breaking down the wooden side-fence. With the hindsight of the knowledge of the 1971 disaster this was a vital factor since the fans on the latter occasion were not able to break down the fence. The fence had been put back in place after the 1961 accident and, it is claimed by some, was strengthened after another accident, in which over thirty were injured, following the Old Firm encounter of 2 January 1969, exactly two years before the disaster.

In September 1967, indeed, there had been yet another incident, after yet another Old Firm match, leading to minor injuries and the twisting of steel handrails installed by Rangers in their extensive re-fashioning of the stairway following the 1961 tragedy. In 1961/2 the club concreted the stairs as well as dividing the exit into seven passageways by means of the rails. Rangers were widely praised for such improvements but, in retrospect, it can be seen that too little attention was paid to the design, as opposed to the condition, of the staircase. The exit was what was termed a 'waterfall staircase', and during the inquest into the 1971 disaster several experts voiced the opinion that the dangers inherent in such a structure might have been minimized by altering the design to create a 'fanning out' effect near the bottom, or that the stairway ought to have been reconstructed into a 'zigzag' style with regular turning points.

Certainly, the serious incidents in 1961, 1967 and 1969 ought to have concentrated the minds of the club's board of directors on the question of the safety of the staircase, more than appeared to be the case from the evidence presented to the inquiry in 1971. The minutes of the meetings of the board of directors that were produced suggest that the issue was neglected, and confirm that the club took no action in 1969 beyond repairing the handrails and fencing that had been damaged. This was in spite of receiving letters of complaint from fans whom, the board minutes indicate, it was decided to 'appease' with complimentary tickets, an offer promptly withdrawn when the club was informed by its insurers that it was not liable for the injuries incurred in the 1969 incident.

As was also made clear at the inquest, Rangers and the police were well aware that stairway 13 was the most popular exit of all those in the stadium. This was on account of its proximity not only to the subway but also to the location of supporters' coaches. It was estimated that over 20,000 would have used the exit in crowds the size of which attended the Old Firm game of 2 January 1971. Rangers had in fact requested a special meeting with the police about matches at Ibrox back in February 1970, but this had been concerned with hooligan behaviour, not safety. During the inquiry in 1971 senior police officers stressed that their interpretation of their role on match days was to curb disorder, and that no effective control could be exercised over departing crowds at exits. The chief superintendent of the Govan division of the Glasgow police stated: 'There is always crushing leaving football matches, normal rushing, they seem to enjoy it and can take it. If we see any person in danger or anyone liable to fall, or anyone being injured through this crushing we would have a duty to act. Until we see this danger we don't act.'

Superintendent Angus MacDonald was forced to acknowledge that the police had a responsibility to prevent dangerous crowd pressure developing and to try to arrange for the crowd to be spread as evenly as possible. It was, however, admitted by his superior that there were no policemen detailed to go to the exit stairways at the end of the game. The priority of the police, as is clear from the inquiry evidence, was the prevention of hooligan behaviour, and many officers were instead instructed after the match to take up positions outside the stadium in case of fighting between rival sets of fans. When it became clear that an accident had occurred on the stairway some officers who remained inside the ground were directed to the top of the terracing to prevent overcrowding at the head of the stairs.

By this time, however, it was too late. As was pointed out by the advocate for the relatives of the deceased at the FAI, the police were admitting responsibility where there was danger to life on the one hand, and on the other saying that they were powerless to control departing crowds. It might be suggested that police could at least have been positioned at the top of the terracing to attempt to spread the departing spectators as evenly as they could down the different lanes of the stairway. The inquiry found that the crowd pressure was far greater in the first three lanes of the stairway looking up, while the ones furthest away from this point were relatively free of crowd pressure.

What became apparent at the FAI was the profound lack of clarity pertaining to the responsibilities held by the police and the club regarding safety, and the ambiguities surrounding the issue of crowd disorder and where it could be said to have overlapped with that of crowd safety. As with the later Hillsborough disaster, there was much confusion of the issues of crowd behaviour and safety. The inquiry into the tragedy in 1961, moreover, had concluded that crowd pressure at the top of the stairs had been the crucial factor in the accident, and a police sergeant who gave evidence agreed that police in future should be stationed at the top of the terracing to control the exit of people. The events of 1971 demonstrated that neither Rangers, nor the police, had absorbed the lessons of the 1961 tragedy, even after the further warnings of 1967 and 1969. The two parties evidently did not purposefully combine to address this specific problem, although relations between them were mutually acknowledged to be excellent, and meetings took place, as noted, about hooliganism.

It should be observed that the police did call a meeting after the 1969 accident when concern over safety was raised. Indeed this meeting was the focus of much attention at the FAI in 1971 and the subsequent court case taken against Rangers. While the police evidence concerning the meeting was presented in a clear and informative fashion, the Rangers officials who were questioned about it were vague in their recollections, and failed to demonstrate that the club took the safety issue seriously enough in the aftermath of the third serious incident on the same stairway. It was this failure, combined with the evidence of the board minutes, which led the Sheriff presiding over the later court case to lambast the club for the manner in which they conducted their business and kept records. The Rangers directors, all of them elderly men out of their depth, cut a pitiful collective figure in the aftermath of the disaster in 1971, and the club's dignity was only salvaged by the organising ability and strength of character shown by the team manager of the time, the legendary Willie Waddell. It would be Waddell's vision of a new Ibrox that would be pursued and eventually realised.

The 1969 meeting about the staircase involved the police, a Rangers director (probably David Hope) and the Glasgow Corporation master of works and his deputy. Ideas were floated about the redesign of the stairway, the replacement of the side fence with handrails was discussed, and the vital issue of crowd pressure at the top of the terracing was addressed in relation to schemes for a tunnel to provide an alternative exit, and the division of the terracing to enforce a more even use of all exits. However, the impression that emerges out of the inquiry evidence is of insufficient agreement being reached as to any one idea, sharp discrepancies between testimonies as to what was suggested and no significant pressure being exerted on Rangers by the police and/or the master of works to adopt a specific scheme to improve safety. There was no follow-up meeting after the 1969 accident before the disaster two years later.

Both the police and the club, as expressed by respective representatives at the inquiry and the court case, were keen to stress the factor of crowd behaviour as something that could not always be predicted. It was said that any measures taken in relation to it could not be assured of success. The consumption of copious amounts of alcohol at the 2 January 1971 match was reflected in the profusion of cans and bottles on the terracing afterwards, yet this was not in itself unusual, and certainly not if the factor of a Scottish New Year was borne in mind. Moreover, the relative absence of alcohol among the victims was clearly recorded at the inquest. Some fans may well have been drunk and this may have influenced their behaviour when departing, but it is doubtful that it was more than a peripheral cause.

Perhaps more pertinent was the intoxicating drama of the closing moments of the match and the mood of jubilation it produced among the Rangers fans. It might also be recalled that news of Aberdeen's late winner in their match (scored by the former Ranger, Forrest) provided further cause for celebration. Certainly it is important to be aware of the feverish emotions generated by an Old Firm match with all its traditional overtones of tribalism and religiosity. There had, of course, been a long history of violence between the fans of 'Protestant Rangers' and 'Catholic Celtic' and Old Firm matches were often the spark for more general disorder. The scale of the police operation on 2 January 1971 was well in excess of the suggested measures for the management of such a crowd contained in the report of the Lang Inquiry into football crowd behaviour, which was published in 1969. Ironically, the crowd on the day was exceptionally well-behaved with police making only three arrests for drunken conduct. Before the incident-packed climax it was being considered as one of the quietest Old Firm contests in the history of the fixture. Such, though, was the ecstatic mood of the fans exiting the Rangers end that the testimonies of eyewitnesses concerning the significance of this factor in the disaster's occurrence have to be given weight. Exiting the stadium was a hazardous business even if the mood of the crowd was sober.

Yet it must be reiterated that there had been precedents. The circumstances of the 1961 fatal accident bore an uncanny resemblance to that of 1971. On the former occasion the departing Rangers fans were in a similarly rapturous mood after a late goal. In 1967 and 1969 the fans were in celebratory spirits following victory over their greatest rivals. Once more it is difficult not to draw the conclusion that Rangers and the police should have addressed more seriously the potential problems that the large exiting crowd posed, especially if happenings on the field had created a mood conducive to recklessness. Again it is pertinent to ask why the problem of crowd pressure at the top of the stairway, identified in the FAI of 1961, was not thoroughly investigated.

The complacency arguably shown by Rangers and the police was, however, symptomatic of a wider culture of neglect and ignorance of football crowds at the level of state policy-formation and decision-taking. The Scottish Office displayed a lack of knowledge about football; pejorative notions about fans and their behaviour inhibited proper evaluation of problems of crowd safety and the question of whether football grounds should be licensed. In the post-war era, notwithstanding the warning delivered by the Bolton disaster, there was a lack of urgency around the matter. The buck, in effect, was passed from the Scottish Office to the Scottish Football Association and then to the clubs themselves. No legislation was passed to force clubs to take safety measures, and this in turn reflected the absence of a consensus of opinion in Britain regarding standards of ground safety. In Scotland, moreover, the Scottish Office habitually confused the issues of crowd behaviour and safety and was mesmerized by the law-and-order ramifications of the Old Firm rivalry. Just six months before the disaster of 1971 a licensing system for Scotland's football grounds was ruled out on the advice of senior civil servants. They maintained that the time was not right for legislation and indicated that such a system would not do anything substantial to prevent the consequences of 'loss of control' and 'panic'. It was doubted that a licensing system would make any significant contribution towards controlling hooliganism and improving crowd behaviour.

The findings of the FAI into the Ibrox disaster of 1971 spared Rangers, and other parties, from blame. However, in recent years some Rangers fans have identified the then custodians of the club as guilty men. In 1974 the club was condemned as negligent by the Sheriff presiding over a test case brought by the wife of a victim of the 1971 tragedy, and she was awarded over £26,000 in damages. By this time only the club's declared intention to modernise Ibrox saved its image from further ruin.

The victims of the disaster were overwhelmingly adult, male, manual workers. Their occupations reflected Glasgow and west-central Scotland's heavy-industrial character, and indicated the extent to which football remained the working man's pastime in the 1970s. There were welders, platers, panelbeaters, machine operators, sheet-metal workers, plumbers, electricians, boilermakers, fitters and steelworkers; in addition there were several young apprentices of various trades. Of the many witnesses who gave evidence at the FAI, most of whom attended the match and were close to the tragic events, the social profile was identical: overwhelmingly male manual workers, predominantly skilled or semi-skilled. This indeed was the occupational profile associated with Rangers' bedrock support since its emergence as a major force in Scottish football in the late nineteenth century. In *Glasgow in 1901* – a portrait of the city drawn by three authors compositely known as 'James Hamilton Muir' – it is skilled craftsmen who are identified giving raucous support to the club. Analysis of the 1902 Ibrox disaster victims also revealed the largest single category to be skilled manual. Moreover, 1971 may well have been the peak of this strata's concentration among the Rangers support. Research into the club's support in the 1980s showed that the predominance of the manual class in general, and the skilled section of it in particular, had shrunk significantly. This research also found that as the club modernised and improved its facilities, and society's work and leisure structures altered, Rangers drew fans from a wider geographical radius – more white-collar workers and more females.

There was one female victim of the 1971 disaster: Margaret

Ferguson from Stirlingshire, an 18-year-old machinist. But perhaps the most heart-rending aspect of the tragedy, to those uninvolved, was the deaths of five teenage boys, all school friends, from the village of Markinch in Fife. The mother of one of the boys, Peter Easton, contributed movingly to a BBC programme to commemorate the thirtieth anniversary of the disaster.

The Ibrox disaster's impact was felt globally, a point made by the Rangers physiotherapist of the time, Tom Craig, in the television documentary. It reverberated throughout the Scottish diaspora, perhaps especially in Canada and Australia. In addition, it profoundly affected the thousands of Rangers supporters in nearby Northern Ireland, the province at this juncture in the midst of its own agonies of political violence and sectarian carnage.

A song in honour of the victims was penned shortly after the disaster by the Scottish folk-singer Matt McGinn who was from an Irish Catholic background. It proclaimed 'the Old Firm united' and 'no Billy, no Dan' and its first verse ran as follows:

New Year bells had been ringing
All Scotland was singing
The old year had died and the new had been born
As the news of disaster, from Ibrox came spreading
The news that would cause a whole nation to mourn.

In the immediate aftermath of the tragedy there were indeed signs of a softening of the Old Firm rivalry. The joint efforts of the two clubs encouraged supporters to make conciliatory gestures. Players and officials of both clubs attended memorial church services for the victims at St. Andrew's Roman Catholic Cathedral and at Glasgow Cathedral. Both clubs gave generously to the Lord Provost of Glasgow's Disaster Fund, and later in January took part as a Rangers and Celtic 'select' team in a special match in aid of the fund held at Hampden Park, Scotland's national stadium. Willie Waddell's swift organisational response ensured that Rangers were represented at every funeral where their presence was welcomed. His handling of the world's media was also impressive. 'His every interview carried strength and understanding', wrote the sports broadcaster Archie Macpherson in his revealing book, *Action Replays*.

Yet it might be argued that Waddell and Rangers spurned a crucial opportunity effectively to address the issue of sectarianism in Scottish football. In relation to Rangers it was a moment when they could have declared their intention to sign Catholic players as well as Protestants. The club had come under pressure to do this since the late 1960s, against a background of changing social and cultural values, practices and attitudes. Had he been as forward-thinking on this matter as on the reconstruction of the stadium, Waddell could have used the latitude his powerful personality afforded him to bring the club truly into a new era. Certainly, he had earned the right to direct the club as he chose, and the times could not have been more propitious in view of the impact of the tragedy.

However, Waddell chose to behave as defiantly over the issue as the Rangers directors then and before. He denied that sectarianism was practised by the club and concentrated instead on eradicating the problem of hooliganism which he regarded as a separate matter. In this he failed. The hooligan behaviour actually worsened, tarnishing the club's reputation and occasions such as its greatest achievement in winning the European Cup Winners' Cup in Barcelona in 1972. To the discomfort of the Rangers management the issue of hooliganism continued to be connected to the club's all-Protestant image by the media. After further trouble at a match in Birmingham in 1976 Waddell stated that Rangers intended to sign players of all faiths. No such signing was made until that of the promising schoolboy John Spencer in the early 1980s (and Spencer indeed went on to make many first-team appearances); however, the practice was not widely acknowledged to have changed until the sensational acquisition of ex-Celtic player Maurice Johnston by the then manager Graeme Souness in 1989. By this time Rangers had much to live down in the eyes of those outside the traditionally minded of their support, although the catalogue of refusals on the part of Catholics pursued by Souness from 1986 indicated how entrenched were the outlooks of many across the divide. Moreover, the perpetuation of sectarian tensions in Scotland might be said to be the outcome of many other factors besides the symbolism of Rangers.

Any hopes of the disaster's impact diminishing sectarian bitterness over the long term were revealed as fanciful as early as May 1971, at the next Old Firm meeting. This Scottish Cup final, watched by over 120,000 at Hampden, produced an 'Orange versus Green' affair every bit as 'traditional' as before the tragedy.

The next Rangers home game following the disaster in 1971 took place as scheduled two weeks later. Stairway 13 was closed and the atmosphere among the smaller than usual crowd of 26,000 was sombre. It would be some weeks before the traditional vibrancy of the terracing returned and, for some, things would simply never be the same again. There are many testimonies of fans who decided to give up attending matches. It was as if such fans took the view that they had literally been flirting with death on a weekly basis and that the time had come to take no more such risks. Meanwhile the issue of crowd pressure at the top of the terracing was finally tackled by means of the construction of a wall to break the flow of spectators, and the wooden side-fences of stairway 13 – which was shortly afterwards renumbered – were replaced by handrails. The stairway was reopened later that season and no accidents were reported between then and the demolition of the terracing to make way for a new stand in 1978.

As the years passed it seemed that the Ibrox disaster was destined to be quietly forgotten, at least in terms of public recognition and visible reminders. Indeed, the disaster was invoked more often in an offensive fashion by some who were antagonistic to Rangers, particularly Celtic fans and, from the 1980s, by followers of

Aberdeen. The latter twist was ironic in the light of the manner in which Rangers fans had sung in praise of the Dons on the fateful day of 2 January 1971. The disaster – like that of the Manchester United Munich air crash of 1958 and other tragedies – itself fell victim to squalid supporters' rivalries.

However, commemoration of a well-meaning and respectful kind came to the fore as the culture of mourning underwent radical change in Britain in the 1980s and 1990s. Pivotal here was the reaction to the Hillsborough disaster of 1989 and the visual demonstration of tokens and symbols of supporters' grief. By the time of the twentieth anniversary of Ibrox many Rangers supporters were beginning to put pressure on the club to honour the memory of the victims. The line taken by the club for many years – that the new Ibrox stadium was in itself a memorial to those who lost their lives – was regarded increasingly by fans as inadequate. On 2 January 1991, when Rangers again faced Celtic at Ibrox, the fans paid their own tributes by laying scarves and other mementoes at the disaster site. A commemorative plaque – organised by the management of the club in response to popular demand – was also unveiled at this corner of the stadium, although the man who ought to have performed the ceremony, Willie Waddell, was absent. A minute's silence was then held before the match started, but a sizeable minority of Celtic supporters interrupted it with jeers and offensive chants. Celtic's subsequent attempt to make light of their fans' show of hatred and bigotry did not receive the media condemnation it warranted, and only served to embitter still further relations between the two sets of fans.

The continuing pressure exerted by supporters for a more prominent and visible memorial finally resulted in the commission of a statue that was unveiled at a special commemorative service at Ibrox to mark the thirtieth anniversary in 2001. The statue was of the club captain of the period, John Greig, who still recalls 2 January 1971 as the worst day of his life. Opinions differ as to whether a statue of a player, however much of a club legend, was the most appropriate tribute. However, there was consensus around the decision to make the memorial in honour not only of the victims of the 1971 disaster, but also of those of 1902 and 1961. 'The players, managers and directors come and go', wrote the editor of the Rangers supporters' fanzine *Follow Follow* at the time of the statue's unveiling, 'but the faceless and nameless crowd is the raw material out of which the club is made. Sadly those who died in the Disasters did not remain faceless and nameless. Remember them all and the reasons why they died.'

The Ibrox disaster of 1971 reflected the fact that British football stadia of the period were, in general, dangerous places. Ibrox was a typical example of a ground that had taken shape at the beginning of the twentieth century and which housed huge numbers of fans with the provision of minimal standards of spectator safety and comfort. If anything, Ibrox was one of the better-appointed grounds, and Rangers could not be said to have neglected in any way the maintenance and condition of the stadium. Nevertheless, too little thought was given to the question of safety, particularly in relation to exiting the ground, when warning had been served in the form of previous accidents on the same stairway.

The disaster also assumes a more singular character when it is borne in mind that it happened after an Old Firm game, as indeed had the previous accidents. The unique character and atmosphere of this fixture cannot be detached from the tragic events, and the disaster's impact on the Old Firm rivalry was significant, if not the catalyst towards change that was widely hoped for by civic society in Scotland. Moreover, a perception of the disaster outside Scotland as resulting from quasi-religious passions with no parallel elsewhere in Britain may have prevented a more attentive appreciation of the lessons that might have been learnt from it in relation to crowd safety in England.

A study of the disaster also helps to shed light on the social composition of the football crowds of the time, and indicates that the early 1970s was probably the last point at which a particular social strata – that of skilled manual workers – so dominated the culture of football crowds, at least in the case of Rangers.

The Ibrox disaster has been much more the subject of popular inquiry and personal remembrance since the late 1980s than before. Partly this reflects the popularity of new technology and the extent to which the internet has allowed more supporters to participate in discussion and reminiscence; yet the main factor seems to have been the general trend towards more explicit displays of commemoration in Scotland and in Britain as a whole, which was clearly visible in fans' reaction to the Hillsborough disaster.

From a personal perspective I welcome the way the disaster has been revisited by a new generation of supporters and the memories of the victims honoured. This has been done in a respectful and dignified fashion and without dodging the hard issues relating to the club's past failings. However, this whole process has been very much driven from the bottom up, with supporters pressurising the club to act. It is a good example of how the soul of the club lies essentially with the fans and the way they choose to guard its name.

A note on sources and further reading

The report of proceedings of the Fatal Accident Inquiry into the Ibrox disaster, and material relating to the compensation case brought against Rangers, are contained in a special Ibrox Disaster archive located in the Mitchell Library, Glasgow. This is the main source on which this study is based. The police evidence is held in Strathclyde Regional Archives (SR 22/51).

In addition to those books referred to in the text, Simon Inglis's *Football Grounds of Britain* is invaluable for Ibrox's history; Bill Murray's *The Old Firm: Sectarianism, Sport and Society in Scotland* is the authoritative academic account of the Rangers–Celtic rivalry;

Callum Brown's article 'Sport and the Scottish Office in the Twentieth Century' in J. A. Mangan (ed.), *Sport in Europe: Politics, Class, Gender* is instructive regarding policy formation; and John Williams, *Seven Years On: Glasgow Rangers and Rangers Supporters 1983–90* contains much information on the profile of Rangers supporters in the period specified.

Several issues of both the Rangers fanzine *Follow Follow* and *The Rangers Historian* contain valuable reflections and discussion.

6

THE BATTLE OF HAMPDEN

Ronnie Esplin

Legendary commentator Archie Macpherson's unmistakable voice, which boomed during coverage of the 1980 Old Firm Scottish Cup final at Hampden, 'There's another charge from the Rangers end', could have signalled the enthusiastic if somewhat unsophisticated style of play for which the Ibrox club were known at that time.

In fact, it was a shocked Macpherson watching a battle between Celtic and Rangers fans unfold before him on the famous Mount Florida turf after the Parkhead side had won the trophy courtesy of George McCluskey's goal in extra time.

In glorious Technicolor, the Hampden Riot, as it became known, confirmed to the world that the age-old enmity between Scotland's two sporting tribes was alive and, literally, kicking.

Footage from that extraordinary episode still makes for compelling viewing. On a gloriously sunny day on Glasgow's south side, a cast of hundreds – most of them young, long-haired, alcohol-fuelled males, dressed in the fashion of the day which included flared trousers, wide-collared shirts and tank tops, with scarves tied around wrists – re-enacted their own contemporary Battle of the Boyne.

Describing the unprecedented scenes to millions of mesmerized viewers throughout the world, a recoiling Macpherson condemns the perpetrators, highlighting the 'pandemonium' and 'turmoil' he sees before him before blurting out what would have appeared obvious to even the most uninformed observer, 'don't kid ourselves, these people hate each other'.

As the mayhem continues unabated for several minutes, a threadbare police presence, almost lost amongst the rampaging supporters but backed by a handful of colleagues on horseback, makes random arrests whilst numerous bottles and other missiles fly vehemently through the air, their destination chillingly unknown.

After one policeman is seen confiscating a huge wooden piece of fencing from a rather confused-looking fan, the television cameras cut to the late Rangers winger Davie Cooper, heading a posse of Ibrox players collecting their losers' medals. The Scottish international looks around as he descends the main-stand stairs, startled by what he sees below him.

When the dust had settled, there was a casualty list of one hundred – four of them policemen – with fifty needing hospital treatment. In total, there were 210 arrests, 160 of which were inside the ground; mere figures, however, that do little justice to the disorder prevalent on that infamous day.

Twenty-five years on, Macpherson reflects on what was an astonishing end to a showpiece occasion: 'It was such a shock because it was so unexpected. There was no indication, suddenly it was just happening in front of me. I just took it as it came, there were no instructions and I spoke off the top of my head. We just had to let it happen and eventually it subsided and the crowd was cleared off the pitch.'

As it turned out, the riot was a watershed not only for Rangers and Celtic but also for Scottish football as a whole. However, given both clubs' form in the hooligan stakes prior to what was their twelfth meeting in the Scottish Cup final, as well as the traditional bitterness between their respective supporters, should we have been surprised about the events that day at Hampden?

There is a long and tawdry history of poor crowd behaviour in Scotland since the time of the original supporters' organisations, the brake clubs, much of it concerning supporters of the Glasgow giants. Indeed, Old Firm fans 'starred' in the only other riot at Hampden back in 1909 in which, according to reports, around 6,000 spectators beat up police, tore down goalposts, lit bonfires and cut firemen's hoses, resulting in fifty-eight police officers and sixty others being treated in hospital. However, significantly, the trouble was not between the Celtic and Rangers fans, but rather was due to the frustrations of both sets of fans at the drawn final having to be replayed; a decision that would have cost them the price of another ticket for Hampden. Unsurprisingly, the cup was withheld that season.

However, this unlikely Old Firm alliance soon dissolved. Sectarianism slowly became entrenched at both clubs and, between 1909 and 1980, there was intermittent disorder and violence at games between and involving both sides. Simple bigotry, although increasingly a major contributory factor to trouble, was not always the catalyst, that dubious honour going to the alcohol-induced, macho terracing culture that became so much a part of watching football in Scotland.

It was the norm for the overwhelmingly male, working class crowds to take a 'cairry-oot' to matches. On a good day, the course and often black humour would be evident but when frustrations were high, the bottles and cans often took on the guise of missiles, mostly to the detriment of fellow fans at the bottom of the terraces.

It would be disingenuous, though, to suggest that as Scottish football left the 1970s it was in the grip of a hooligan epidemic or that things would spiral out of control the way they would in England. However, regular domestic tribulations had stacked up over the years and, by the spring of 1980, several outbreaks of disorder involving Old Firm fans, especially on their travels, were relatively fresh in the mind.

Rangers were still trying to come to terms with the post-match trouble that tarnished the Ibrox club's 1972 European Cup Winners' Cup win in Barcelona, and which had prevented them defending the trophy. Some unrepentant Gers fans subsequently took their misplaced sense of Caledonian bravado on a tour of England, first to Manchester United in 1974 and then to Birmingham in 1976 for a 'friendly' with Aston Villa. Both trips ended with vicious altercations on and off the pitch between the Scots and opposition supporters. An increasingly emboldened Scottish media held the Ibrox club to account especially after Birmingham, mostly on charges of sectarianism which the club continued to refute, but also asking for other offences at Wolverhampton and Newcastle in the 1960s to be taken into consideration.

Journalist Ian Archer, who took particular delight in making the Ibrox club squirm – knowing the Rangers boardroom was racked by guilt – was moved to write the most stinging of condemnations in his *Glasgow Herald* column. It still rankles with many Gers fans to this day: 'This has to be said about Rangers . . . as a Scottish football club they are a permanent embarrassment and an occasional disgrace. This country would be a better place if Rangers did not exist.'

Celtic fans had less of a troublesome reputation on their travels than their city rivals, although the frustration of losing to Liverpool in the semi-final of the European Cup Winners' Cup at Anfield in 1965 led to a particularly spectacular bottle-launch on the famous Spion Kop. However, the Parkhead supporters' indiscretions had been more recent than their Ibrox counterparts. In 1979 Celtic had been embarrassed by their fans during an Anglo-Scottish Cup defeat at Burnley, the ugly incident recalled with some trepidation by one correspondent to a Turf Moor website: 'The atmosphere was simply hostile from the start, it looked as though the Celtic fans were there for no other reason than to cause trouble. The fence separating home and away fans on the 'Longside' was being ripped up and a full-scale riot looked on the cards.'

If some Old Firm fans were hell-bent on displaying their religious identities and divisions through violence, at least the players, while enduring the pressures of life in either blue or green, had learned to live with each other in a more harmonious way. Former Rangers striker, and now BBC pundit, Gordon Smith, recalls the intensity generated in his first game against Celtic after signing for the Govan club in the summer of 1977. At the same time he reveals the differing attitudes of players and fans:

> In my first Old Firm game I ran to take a throw in over at the Jungle side of Parkhead. I just looked up and what a fright I got, there were thousands of people wanting to kill me and I thought they would have if they could have got over the barrier. But we never thought we were representing the Protestant tradition. Nobody talked about that in the dressing room. In fact we joked that Celtic's 'proddy' players would have to play better to get into their team. But the players got on fine, there were no problems at all and in the three years I was at Ibrox the first time it never got out of hand once on the pitch. Johnny Doyle lived around the corner from me in Kilmarnock and he was always in my house. In one game he tackled me and I got up pointing a finger at him and saying, 'that's it, you're not coming round to my house for tea again' and he was pointing back at me and saying, 'I don't want to come round, your tea's rubbish.' I laughed after the game when my wife told me the radio had said we had been fighting; I knew what they were talking about. I think we saw ourselves in the same light; we had more in common with each other than we did with players of other teams.

The Old Firm's unique rivalry, however, has not evolved in a societal vacuum, therefore it is perhaps worth noting the sub-plots that impinged on the final of 1980. The Irish influence at both clubs had increased over the years since stricter demarcation lines had been drawn up around the time of the first world war, firming up after the 'Troubles' hit the headlines in 1969. The stone-throwing images from grainy black-and-white television pictures at that time had been watched mostly with bemusement in Scotland. However, the conflict in Northern Ireland gradually moved to a more sinister level and the ripples from each new wave of atrocity in the Province had nudged the uneasy equilibrium among the more 'traditional' Old Firm fans further out of kilter. The highly publicised IRA hunger strikes in 1981 would do much to crank up the tensions in the west of Scotland even further.

According to the SFA's security chief, Willie McDougall – a former policeman who was on duty at the final – the crucial decision to station most of the officers outside Hampden for the match finishing, was not without reason:

> There had been Loyalist and Republican trials at the High Court in Glasgow around then so our strategy was to try and keep a lid on that. We thought it was alright to let them shout at each other inside the stadium, at least it was not shooting or bombings which could have happened given the Irish influence on both sides of the divide at that time. Our policy was to try and ensure the general public was protected from anti-social behaviour so we had to look at the flashpoints outside the ground.

As Britain bathed in the long spring heatwave of 1980, political problems were not confined to simmering tensions across the water. A new industrial revolution of sorts was about to arrive and Scotland was valiantly resisting the changes that would ultimately take the working classes from coal face to call centre, from steelworks to service sector. The Winter of Discontent in 1978–9, which saw unemployment levels soar to record heights, helped bring down the Labour government. Margaret Thatcher's controversial tenure as Conservative prime minister was in its infancy and at the same time as she declared to the blue-rinse brigade at the annual Tory conference, 'I look forward to the creation of more jobs', the Iron Lady was, in fact, gearing up to go into battle with the trade unions, with Scotland set to suffer disproportionately in the ensuing carnage.

The various branches of the media were dominated by stories of industrial unrest. Scottish teachers were complaining about their unpaid extra-curricular activities, the Talbot car workers were on strike down south ready to be joined by farmers, print unions and the steel workers. Amidst all that, Old Firm supporters were reading that a carefully-timed bus drivers' strike on the day of the game would affect their journey to Hampden.

As far as most football fans were concerned, though, the upheaval and unrest in British society was overshadowed by welcome changes in the natural football order in Scotland. For the first time in decades the Old Firm had been supplanted as the country's best teams as the New Firm of Dundee United and Aberdeen came to the fore in what was turning out to be the most successful period in their histories.

Jim McLean's Dundee United had won the League Cup, the club's first major honour. Then Alex Ferguson's Aberdeen had secured their first-ever Premier League title in the midweek before the Scottish Cup final with a 1–1 draw at Partick, the only occasion on which the title had left Glasgow since Kilmarnock won it in 1964/65. For the first time in living memory, Celtic and Rangers – managed by two legendary former captains, Billy McNeill and John Greig respectively – were struggling to cope with new challengers in what was traditionally a two-horse race. However, it was Greig who was under most pressure going into the Hampden final. The Parkhead side had already qualified for the UEFA Cup through their league position but Rangers would fail to qualify for Europe for only the third time since European football began in the mid-fifties if they failed to lift the trophy.

Greig, though, may have been quietly confident given his recent Scottish Cup record as Light Blues boss. After winning the competition in the previous two seasons, beating Aberdeen and Hibs in the finals of 1978 and 1979, the Ibrox club were going for three-in-a-row and were thought by most pundits to be favourites. Celtic's early season form had deserted them; in April they had lost twice at home to Aberdeen as well as losing 3–0 at Tannadice and 5–1 at Dens Park.

In addition, the loss of centre backs Roddy McDonald and Tom McAdam through suspension was a huge blow for McNeill who had to conjure up an untried defensive duo to deal with the aerial threat of Derek Johnstone. Roy Aitken would move back to defence with the relatively unknown Mike Conroy and, in a reshuffled Parkhead side, winger Davie Provan was playing in an unfamiliar midfield role. The Ibrox club were, ostensibly, in better shape missing only the services of the ineligible midfielder Ian Redford, although there were doubts over defender Tom Forsyth.

The blazing sunshine that was enveloping Scotland added an edge to what was always going to be a highly charged occasion. Journalist Hugh Keevins, then working for *The Scotsman*, recalls the atmosphere in the surrounding environs as he made his way to Hampden that afternoon. He said: 'It was a scorcher of a day and when I was going up to the game through the south side of Glasgow, pubs like Heraghtys were heaving and the fans were outside in the street with their pints.'

However, as the supporters rolled up to Hampden there was no hint of what was about to unfold. Hooliganism had always been opportunistic, as opposed to organised, although big games in Mount Florida had always caused some problems for locals. David Wilson, secretary of the Mount Florida community council, in what had become a familiar theme, wrote a letter to the *Glasgow Herald* pointing out: 'We all dread Old Firm matches. Some people just pack up and go away for the weekend and others lock themselves into their houses. . . . Let's hope for once that the fans behave themselves.'

The fans paid the princely sum of £2 and £2.50 for their terracing tickets in what was to be Hampden's last big game before a major revamp in the summer. The attendance of 70,303 was well up on the disappointing 54,252 who saw the previous Old Firm Scottish Cup final three years earlier, but paltry when compared to the massive 122,714 who watched the same two teams compete in the 1973 final.

Those supporters who forked out forty pence for their match programme were rewarded with a deliciously prescient interview with Ernie Walker, then secretary of the SFA. On the problems of hooliganism, Walker said: 'Football cannot cure the problem but it must do everything possible to contain it . . . more seats would help . . . moving in this direction.' As well as fans being encouraged by advertisements in the programme to invest in the new high-tech Betamax video player, the virtues of Eldorado wine, Famous Grouse whisky and Youngers Tartan Special were extolled. Not that the punters needed much encouragement. The ritual 'cairry oot' was not to be forsaken because of pre-match warnings not to bring drink into the stadium. Optimistic notices at the turnstiles informing supporters that, 'cans and bottles cannot be taken into the ground' were ignored and with police unable by law to search the fans, it was simply a case of hiding booze up jumpers or in jacket pockets.

Arguably the fans needed to dull the senses to enjoy the half-time entertainment which, in contrast to the pomp and ceremony of a traditional Wembley cup final, was more of a testament to Scottish kitsch. A penalty shoot-out between a collection of entertainers that included Andy Cameron, Mr Abie, the Alexander Brothers and Johnny Beattie would complement beautifully – someone must have thought – the Snohomish High School marching band from Washington state in the American north-west, which was on its way to performing what would be its most memorable gig.

Celtic's starting eleven was shaped with attack in mind:

Latchford, Sneddon, Aitken, Conroy, McGrain, Provan, McLeod, Burns, Doyle, McCluskey, McGarvey. On the bench were Davidson and Lennox, the veteran substitute providing the last link with the Lisbon Lions of 1967.

Rangers' worries over Forsyth proved to be unfounded and they lined up as expected: McCloy, Jardine, Forsyth, Jackson, Dawson, Stevens, Russell, Smith, Cooper, Johnstone, McDonald. Including substitutes McLean and Miller, there were six players involved from the European Cup Winners' Cup-final squad in Barcelona eight years previously.

Referee George Smith was taking charge of his first cup final as well as his first Old Firm meeting and, ironically, he was involved in a fairly unremarkable afternoon until he blew the final whistle. Rangers had the best of the early stages, with winger Davie Cooper the pick of the Ibrox men, but Greig's side struggled to create much with Conroy, arguably the Hoops' best player, blunting the aerial threat of Johnstone. Celtic, however, rallied and came back into the match but although there were chances at both ends as the game went on, there were no complaints when the match ended in a stalemate.

It looked likely that the first goal would win it and the break-through eventually came after 107 minutes when Rangers defender Ally Dawson headed out a corner to Celtic full back Danny McGrain on the edge of the crowded Gers penalty area. When the Scottish international's harmless-looking shot came back towards goal, keeper Peter McCloy looked to have it covered until Hoops striker McCluskey stuck out a leg and redirected it into the opposite corner of the goal.

While the Ibrox men battled in vain for an equaliser, most fans would not have noticed the vast majority of police inside the ground being reassigned to potential flashpoints outside. Stewarding of games in those days was minimal, low-key and haphazard; effectively 70,000 fans were left all but unattended. It was that crucial decision to redeploy police, explained by McDougall earlier, which facilitated the initial pitch invasion. However, in the dying moments of a typically hard-fought Old Firm game there was no indication of anything untoward.

Indeed, as soon as the final whistle went and the roar went up from the Celtic half of the stadium, many, if not most, of the dejected Rangers fans quickly made their way down the steep Hampden stairs and out of the exits. Thousands of those supporters then made their way home, oblivious to the events they would only learn about later.

George Wells recalls the confusion among many bluenoses:

I left the game at the final whistle and I would say about 75 per cent of fellow Rangers fans did likewise. We were walking up towards Cathcart Road to get the supporters' bus and heard Rangers fans singing, 'Hello, Hello' fairly loudly, we thought, considering the number of fellow supporters that had left the park. The first sign of something being wrong was when numerous police officers were attempting to run contra-flow through the crowd back towards Hampden. Then we saw two abandoned police cars being vandalised, one eventually turned over on its side. When we had an unusually long wait on the bus everyone then started clicking that something was amiss. There was traffic chaos, total gridlock and then some fellow supporters from our bus arrived back very late to inform us of the trouble that had taken place. Funny enough, I spoke to a friend a number of years later about that day and he recalled he was working in Hamburg at the time. He was playing pool in a bar with the telly on in the background and he was amazed to suddenly hear a huge chorus of the 'Billy Boys' – it was the start of the six o'clock German news.

As those Rangers supporters who had stayed behind watched on, the victorious Hoops players went to the Celtic end to take the acclaim of their fans. Photographer Richard Parker, working for the *Sunday Mail* that day, takes up the story:

> The photographers were all together in a huddle at the end of the game waiting for Celtic to go up for the cup. I looked round and saw one Celtic fan run up to the centre circle and gesture to the Rangers end. Then three Rangers fans came on followed by twenty supporters from the Celtic end and then about fifty from the Rangers end. It was like watching a game of tennis as the fans came on from both ends and we were stuck in the middle of it all. We were in shock; it was incredible, it was two sides going to war. We began taking pictures and there was some 'handbags' between the fans but there was some real violence as well. One colleague – who I don't want to name, but who had a short fuse – was taking some pictures when a Rangers fan came up and kicked him hard in the shin. It looked a sore one and the photographer dropped his other camera off his shoulder, swung it up in the air and then down on to this guy's head. The fan was carried off on a stretcher and then the photographer was going round looking for bits of his smashed camera on the pitch.

Celtic fan Eddie Docherty and his party watched from the back of the uncovered east terracing:

> I went along to the final with my mate, his two older brothers and a couple of their friends. Also joining us was my mate's cousin, visiting from South Africa, who was excited about going to his first Old Firm game. The match itself was pretty forgettable apart, of course, from the goal in extra time. At the final whistle the Celtic team came over to our end to do the scarf-collecting, hat-wearing thing. A few fans, young fans it looked from where we were standing, ran on to the

park towards the end of the team's celebration and then a few older fans ran on. By this stage the Rangers end, from what I can remember, looked empty. But the next thing there were some Rangers fans on the pitch as well. There was clearly some aggro but to be honest, we all saw it as bit of a joke and were laughing at the whole thing. There was then a charge by Celtic fans towards the Rangers fans and then back again. While it was clearly becoming more serious, we still saw it more in comedy terms and the arrival of the police horses only added to the entertainment. As we were leaving, it became clear the real trouble was outside the ground. I remember looking to my right as we were about to descend the stairs from the Celtic end, to see this cloud of dust in front of the main stand and a running battle under it. That looked much nastier than anything on the pitch. I think we all thought the same as one of our crowd said we should all go back to his house, which was near Hampden, until things calmed down. We had a few drinks and watched the riot on the news. It looked much worse than I'd remembered it and Archie Macpherson's, 'lets face it these people hate each other' comment just added to the on-screen gravity which I certainly hadn't felt at the ground.

The Old Firm players, unsurprisingly, had mixed experiences. Celtic keeper Peter Latchford still vividly remembers the aftermath: 'I was behind the goal, facing the Celtic fans and applauding them. I noticed the crowd reaction changing and I turned round and saw the Rangers fans coming at us. I was off! It was the fastest I moved all afternoon!'

Although Davie Cooper watched the skirmishes from the trophy podium, teammate Smith somehow managed to miss the pitched battle: 'We were shepherded off the pitch and we sat in the dressing room talking about the game. Then we went up for our medals and I was so disappointed I never lifted my head up. I was back in the dressing room and hadn't noticed it. The players were talking about it and I didn't know what they were on about.'

As fans clashed all over the pitch, mounted police arrived in an effort to drive the intruders back over the fences. Young Elaine Murdie, a woman police constable, got her fifteen minutes of fame charging around on a grey police horse trying to restore order. This was in stark contrast to the only time mounted police were ever needed at the English Cup final: when a lone white horse gently pushed back the well-behaved overspill during the 1923 final at the new Wembley. However, despite the best efforts of Murdie and her colleagues the charge and counter-charges between the two sets of fans continued for several minutes as the bulk of the police presence came scrambling back from their duty points outside the stadium. The famous old Hampden goals were being used akin to a field hospital and pictures would show a young boy crying in the back of the net at the Rangers end while a St Andrews ambulance person attended to an injured fan, probably a relative.

All the while, sitting transfixed at the front of the main stand, were the American visitors from the Snohomish High School marching band.

The *Daily Record's* photographer that day, Eric Craig, was one of the afternoon's most serious casualties. Now retired, he blames the policing strategy for his injury:

> I still remember it vividly. It was a major blunder by the police. If it hadn't been for the mounted police, there would have been corpses on either side. I was on the pitch taking photos of assaults, punch-ups and there was no problem. I wasn't frightened; I had been at Newcastle and Barcelona so I knew what to watch for. But the riot had finished and I started to pack my equipment away at the Rangers end when it happened. I got hit by a half-full Pomagne bottle of all things and received a depressed fracture of my skull. I

was off work for four or five months and I ended up 90 per cent deaf in my right ear.

There was to be no lap of honour after the Celtic players eventually collected the cup and their medals and Peter Latchford is still annoyed that what should have been a glory day had been spoiled:

You won this damned cup and you want to go out and celebrate. Not only had you beat your biggest rivals, you want to go and rub their faces in it, of course you do and make sure they know but we couldn't do it. The fact that we couldn't do a lap of honour still rankles with me. I won the Scottish Cup three times and I was never allowed to go round Hampden with it. We were stopped from going all the way round in 1975 against Airdrie when Billy McNeill was captain and playing his last game and in 1977 against Rangers we were also banned from parading it. It wasn't a nice feeling in 1980 because, when you win it, you want to stay out there and enjoy it. We couldn't and there was a lot of mumping and moaning in the dressing room about that. We went back to the Celtic Park boardroom with all the wives and hangers-on but the mood was one of annoyance and the other lads probably felt the same as me.

The soul-searching began as the Scottish nation tried to come to terms with what it had witnessed. The immediate aftermath, though, was almost as ugly as proceedings on the pitch as all sides tried to distance themselves from any blame. Unsurprisingly, the police accepted no criticism and planted the blame quickly and firmly at the Parkhead door. So did SFA president Jack Harkness, who declared, 'what sparked off the invasion was some Celtic players going up to the Celtic end. They should never have been allowed.' This was despite the fact that some reports subsequently suggested the Parkhead players had, in fact, received permission to go to their fans. George Younger, secretary of state for Scotland, reiterated to the House of Commons that police had, 'blamed drink and the actions of some of the Celtic fans', which served only to exacerbate an already fraught situation.

Rangers battened down the hatches, well aware that their sectarian signing-policy would again be held up for nationwide inspection. From the Ibrox boardroom a cowardly statement emanated that did little to enhance the club's plummeting reputation. In classic head-in-the-sand style the Govan club let it be known that it 'agreed with earlier statements from the Secretary of State and the SFA president.'

While the Rangers board quivered behind closed doors, wishing the world would go away, there was no such reticence from the other side of the city. Celtic chairman Desmond White, a vigorous supporter of the Parkhead club and its fans, regularly enjoyed eating his Ibrox counterparts for breakfast. White was incandescent at what appeared to be a three-pronged attack on his club from Rangers, the police and the SFA: 'They blame us. It annoys me. In fact, it appals me.'

The clubs were more united at supporter level as mouthpieces for the two sets of fans accepted no responsibility for their members' actions. Rangers Supporters Association secretary David Miller was quoted as saying: 'The blame must lie with the chief constable for allowing the invasion to happen', while a spokesman for the Celtic Supporters Association could only mutter that: 'Police were conspicuous by their absence.'

However, the Old Firm and their fans were held accountable by an outraged media that, in truth, were reflecting wider public opinion. Amidst a veritable rainforest of condemnation, Alex Cameron's *Daily Record* column was headed: 'How long must we wait Rangers?' a clear reference to the club's anti-Catholic practices while Hugh Taylor mourned the game in his *Evening Times* piece: 'Why I cry for Scottish football.'

However, the most perceptive and ageless analysis came in Jimmy Reid's column in the *Glasgow Herald*, famously entitled: 'Too many Protestants, Too many Catholics, not enough Christians.' Reid – who made his name as a trade union leader during the Upper Clyde Shipbuilders strikes of the early seventies – castigated the guilty fans as the, 'demoralised dregs of the Clydeside working class . . . the teenagers of last Saturday are products of bigoted parents, or a bigoted social environment or a bigoted church, or all three'. He noted that on the mainland United Kingdom, Scotland was the 'only place where matrimony between two white Caucasian Christians can be described as a mixed marriage'.

Looking for further explanation for the divisiveness in Scottish society – which had manifested itself in spectacular style at the national stadium – Reid also grasped the nettle of the country's segregated education system, 'I appeal to our Catholic friends for some sort of integration.'

Reid's desire for a more inclusive Scotland would fall on deaf ears but football as a spectator sport would never be the same again. Celtic protested at the SFA fine of £20,000, which they incurred along with the Ibrox club, but there were to be longer-lasting repercussions. The Scottish Criminal Justice Act was passed, instantly ending the decades-long booze culture associated with the game in Scotland. No longer could drink or drunks be admitted to a sporting arena and the police had the powers and the backing of the general public to enforce the new law.

The way football matches were to be policed was also subject to review. Chief superintendent John Malcolm, of G division in Glasgow, is currently in charge of policing at Ibrox and Hampden and uses footage of the riot as a briefing tool for his officers. Could an outbreak of disorder ever happen again at a big match in Glasgow? Malcolm thinks not:

It would take something extreme for us to be caught the way we were back in 1980. There are still issues with drink but there has been a change in the public's behaviour. For instance, in one Old Firm game in 2003 we had three arrests, two drink-related and one for throwing a coin. The amount of containers found after the game was negligible and the ones which were alcohol containers were minuscule. Rangers and Celtic fans are used to going to big games in Glasgow and they are used to the new policing system so there's not a lot of trouble at the matches now. And when the Old Firm matches are finished, and I'm specifically talking about Ibrox, Celtic fans will walk peacefully away not attempting to breach the police line which segregates them from the home supporters, unlike at some games in England where confrontation is expected.

Security chief McDougall, who has travelled to matches all over the world in his role with the SFA, agrees that the mindset of those attending big games has changed over the years:

Along with all-seated stadiums, the restriction of drink has been the biggest influence in the improved behaviour of fans in Scotland. I watched an Old Firm game last year in a an ex-pats pub in Perth, Australia and it was like going back forty years in time, such was the vitriolic hatred. I came out thinking 'my God, we've come a long way since then'. Football has had to change and adapt and the expectations are higher now. The days of the bottle in the pocket are gone. We're trying to set up a football experience at Hampden for cup finals as well as Scotland games.

However, a quarter of a century on from that fateful day in Mount Florida, it would be folly to suggest that Old Firm games are now peaceful occasions. The advent of tougher laws on alcohol consumption, more rigid policing, early kick-off times and live television has, amongst other things, resulted in the displacement of violence away from Ibrox, Parkhead and Hampden. The terracing booze-culture has been replaced by the Sky television booze-culture with most of the trouble emanating from pubs and clubs where ticketless fans watch matches. The great paradox is that being at the game is probably the safest place to be when Celtic and Rangers meet.

The fascination with Old Firm tribalism continues. On 27 February 2005, the *Panorama* programme entitled 'Scotland's Secret Shame', was yet another attempt to analyse and discuss the sectarian problems that bedevil the country's two biggest football clubs. Despite the inclusion of several falsehoods – and the adoption of a flawed and sensationalist approach – the programme was, by common consent, a damning indictment of both clubs and their fans. All the violence, bitterness and bigotry that had been on display at Hampden twenty-five years before was revealed to a new generation of viewer. The only real difference these days is that most of the trouble happens away from the stadiums.

Twenty-five years on Gordon Smith admits that the Old Firm hostility continues to dog him:

When Rangers are playing at Parkhead I can feel a different attitude towards me. Other games are fine and I get no hassle and obviously at Ibrox it's okay but it definitely changes on Old Firm day at Celtic Park when I am definitely seen as an ex-Rangers player. I went to Parkhead earlier in the year [2004] and I was a little bit later than usual arriving so I had to park my car at the Celtic shop. It was mobbed there and also over at the main stand as the fans waited on the team buses coming in. As I made my way through the supporters I could hear the comments, 'Orange bastard' and so on but you've just got to go with it. I'm not sure if it's ever going to change and, if it did, would it still be the same game?

7

GRAEME SOUNESS WAS DYNAMITE

Alex Anderson

I know my fate. One day there will be associated with my name the recollection of something frightful, of a crisis like no other before on earth, of the profoundest collision of conscience, of a decision evoked against everything that until then had been believed in, demanded, sanctified. I am not a man. I am dynamite.

(F. W. Nietzsche, *Ecce Homo*)

Spring of 1986. It was a better journey back from Glasgow this Friday night than it was last Saturday evening. There was no sea of green on the platform at Paisley Gilmour Street this time, waiting to spot us and slag us as the Largs train rolled in. No fighting on the train as the Dalry boys let just enough o' the ratbags into our carriage to give a good kicking. They're all lying as low tonight as we were six days ago. We all thought Walter Kidd had equalised for Hearts last Saturday but the tranny listeners at Ibrox were doing a spot of wishful thinking and I just went along with it for a minute or two, like everyone else. Think we all just needed to believe it hadn't really happened. It was bloody ALBERT Kidd, making it 2–0 for DUNDEE. Super Ally's hat-trick tonight was pretty damned real though! Coming to our place to rub their jammy league title down our throats! I

think not – get it rrrright up yese. 'Mickey Mouse Cup!' those bams
shouted at Jasper at Central. Right enough – the Glasgow Cup is a bloody
joke. As was me and Dingy missing the first goal cos the train was late.
As was managing to bump intae Ronnie on the east enclosure – it was
trampolining tonight! As was Peter Latchford in goals for them – didn't
know he was still alive! But that's all hardly the point – Souness isn't
even here for real yet and he's already beat those bams.

'So gentleman, can I just say to you, welcome our new player-
manager – Graeme Souness.' It wasn't the best grammar and, truth
be told, he stuttered on the third word, almost saying 'So gentlemen,
to you I can just say. . . .' David Holmes was a man who tried to
invest his sentences with so much gravitas he often forgot to finish
them. His proclivity for talking about the Holmes family and in
particular his wife Betty as if she was first lady to his president, as
if she was queen to his king, as if anyone cared, was actually
indicative of an astute awareness of what the Rangers fans wanted
– success delivered with the regality of the Struth and Symon reigns.

Just over a year later, the Rangers chairman delivered the second
most memorable line of his life. Speaking direct to the camera on
the Pittodrie trackside he offered a toast to all the Rangers supporters
watching that night's *Sportscene* on BBC Scotland: 'Rangers
Football Club, Premier Division champions 1986/87.' It made me
cry, that toast. Its beautiful simplicity still chokes me when I think
of it today. Our chairman knew what the punters wanted, he knew
he'd delivered it and he knew how to knock home the magnitude
of the achievement. Such theatre needs a man who can deliver his
lines. But the syntax and the dynamics were far from smooth when
he pulled the pin from the grenade that exploded Scottish football.
Even David Holmes almost lost his reverential words when intro-
ducing Souness to the media on 8 April 1986.

Footage of this legendary press conference was shot from two
different cameras at slightly different angles. In one – when Holmes
says those magical words and a side door is opened – Souness

doesn't appear instantaneously. Is he actually there at all, you wonder? From the other angle he emerges from the adjoining backroom pretty quickly but the door shields him from one camera for an agonisingly long number of seconds. Watching at home, we still pondered if it was all a hoax. Perhaps he was just waiting for the dry ice – 'tonight, Matthew, Rangers are going to be a world-renowned football club' – or perhaps it was just too good to be true. After all, Rangers didn't have player-managers, Rangers didn't sign people from Italian clubs, Rangers didn't make the world sit up and take notice. In early 1986, Rangers just didn't do excitement.

But then he's there. In the middle of it all. The camera flashes start popping and, taking his hands out his pockets – he's so cool! – he reciprocates Holmes's 'welcome to the club, Graeme' with an almost inaudible 'thanks, David' and a firm handshake. Graeme Souness's skin colour matches the mahogany of the panelling on the wall far better than the pasty faces of the Rangers officials and world-weary press men all around. A tan honed under a Mediterranean sun, a tight perm of a darkly menacing mane, the moustache that Freddie Mercury probably envied and the ears tucked back by a cosmetic surgeon. His presence in that room is glamour of confrontational proportions. 'Here I stand' said Martin Luther – Souness didn't even bother with the verbal stuff. He just stood. Everyone with a television just gawped . . . even if they weren't watching their televisions!

The crowd booed at the end of our game two days previously. What there was of a crowd at Rangers games had booed a few times down the last eight years. The fact we were losing to Tottenham, in a friendly, was actually a matter of some exoticism. Today, it's easy to forget how bad a state Rangers found themselves in during Jock Wallace's second spell as manager. The campaign Tottenham impinged upon was particularly brutal. Europe had consisted of one tie and one Rangers goal – Pamplona's Athletico Osasuna were the beneficiaries of our charity in the Spanish club's first-ever venture into continental competition. Even our trustworthy League Cup had deserted us, Hibs edging the semi. As the domestic season frittered away, Rangers were struggling to finish fifth in the league.

This was all shameful for a club of our standing but not an entirely new depth. In 1978/79 we suffered a last-gasp championship-decider disappointment to the dying vestiges of the Lisbon Lions. The following season we managed fifth place in a ten-team league, with even St Mirren finishing above us. In fact, in each of the campaigns from 1979 to 1986, we finished no higher than third and no lower than fifth. Fourth place was our usual and, in the days of two points for a win, we were never any closer than eleven points from the champions when the Scottish Football League was dishing out the bunting. We'd won a treble in seventy-eight but since then we'd won two Scottish Cups – both after replays from dreary goalless gala day anti-climaxes – and four League Cups. We did make the European Cup quarter-final as a last hurrah for the Cup Winners' Cup survivors of 1972 but that was on the eve of the eighties. This was 1986 and a few knockout cups on the home front were not enough to keep Ibrox even two-tenths full at times. Even when we did win, it wasn't that great to watch and there was no real underlying hope that it would be sustained for the course of a league campaign.

The aesthetic of Rangers' play changed under Souness. Unsurprisingly, under Greig and then Wallace again, we played a sub-standard remnant of the mid-to-late seventies style, which had reaped rewards through no little skill but massive physical endeavour. This all-action approach was gleaned as much in the sand dunes of Gullane, near ex-commando Wallace's Wallyford birthplace, as it was on the tactics board or the five-a-side pitch. At the peak of their powers these men won domestic trebles and brought Rangers their only European trophy. As they aged, their bodies began to reap the rewards of Wallace's ferocious conditioning. Ibrox playing legends such as Greig, Sandy Jardine, Alex MacDonald, Tom

Forsyth, Peter McCloy, Tommy McLean and Willie Johnston all played top-flight football until they approached their forties. When doing it for Rangers they eventually found themselves employed by a set-up more intent on rebuilding the stadium than the team. As the seventies became the eighties the loyal servants were told by fans they were too old. When doing it for Hearts, having been discarded by Rangers, they often came back to teach those fans some manners.

Bobby Russell and Davie Cooper were the youngest remainders of the 1978 treble-winning team. New men like Ally McCoist, Ian Ferguson, Cammy Fraser and Craig Paterson had all been signed to augment the developing talent from the Ibrox youth system such as Ian Durrant and Dave McPherson. It didn't work. Season 1985/86 remains, to date, the only time in our thirteen-decade history when Rangers lost more games than we won. When we used up so many of those victories in climbing briefly to the summit of the league in September, you can imagine just how ingrained the slump must have been by the following April.

I threw my scarf away. What a tit! I'd thrown my fucking scarf away!! Spending New Year's Day at Parkhead was bad enough but then Paul McGuigan scored and ran up to the Rangers end and blessed himself. Then it had to be Peter bloody Grant, 'Mister Sellik', who made it 2–0. But then Jock Wallace, my managerial hero, takes off Derek Ferguson, my current young playing hero – one of our few hopes for the future. Before I knew what I was doing it all got to me and I couldn't help copying all the part-timer clowns I swore I'd never become. Something my Nana bought me when I was nine years old, when we were last league champions, got lost in a sea of 18,000 Bears. I stayed after the final whistle and scoured the empty terracing but it was gone. Okay, mine is the only Rangers scarf in existence with Red, White AND Blue tassles but, still, what were the chances of me spotting that guy in the bus park with an extra scarf! Felt grateful but ashamed when he gave it back to me saying, 'Don't you EVER do that again'. Those Ulster accents are scary. The following game,

scarf tied safely roon my plukey neck, we beat Dundee 5–0 . . . maybe this
is a sign . . . maybe things are going to change.

It's easy for young fans today, knowing no non-Old Firm team
has won the league in twenty years, to claim Rangers dominate so
much of the current Scottish game purely because of their wealth.
They'll look back at the record books and think the Rangers that
won the league in 1987 did it thanks to the same spending-power
advantage they have today. Yes, the money forked out by Holmes
and Souness was way above anything anyone else was spending,
but the opposition was of a far greater calibre and far wider range
than anything the current Scottish Premier League can offer.

Aberdeen, under the pre-knighthood Alex Ferguson, had been
champions of Scotland in three of the last five years. They retained
the nucleus of the side that lifted the European Cup Winners' Cup
and Super Cup just three years previously. Dundee United, under
the autocratic Jim McLean, were about to reach the UEFA Cup final
during Souness's first full season in Scotland. The Tannadice club
were league champs just three years before, European Cup semi-
finalists the season after that (they would have met a Liverpool
side captained by Souness in his final game for the Anfield club if
they'd overcome AS Roma). Celtic would win the 1985/86 championship, on the last day of the season, pipping on goal difference
a Hearts team which was over a year unbeaten at Tynecastle. At the
age of seventeen I could remember Rangers winning league games
at Pittodrie and Parkhead just once each.

All around me at my Ayrshire school in the early-mid eighties,
my traitorous act of supporting Rangers instead of Ayr United or
Kilmarnock was starting to look pretty tired compared to the growing
number of Aberdeen and Dundee United fans from Ardrossan, Saltcoats and West Kilbride . . . none of whom had ever been to Pittodrie
or Tannadice once. I'd visited both a good few times and Pittodrie, in
particular, epitomised the Rangers rut; one cold January, I watched
Frank McDougall rattle in four as the Dons did us by five goals to one.

'You Gotta Fight for Your Right to Party' was climbing the charts by the time we were topping the league in March 1987, but it took Souness one whole season before he could guide us to a win on Grampian and two before we left Parkhead with all the points. However, as with the very arrival of the man himself, these wins were stamped with *apres moi le deluge*. Souness was the first-ever player-manager of Rangers and he was the first Rangers manager to ever knowingly sign a Roman Catholic. As the years went on and more and more Catholic men played in Rangers royal blue to less and less incredulity, we found ourselves winning at Aberdeen and Celtic at least once a season, sometimes twice. Ten years after the Souness revolution, Walter Smith won all four league encounters with Celtic. The previous season he'd won both trips to Pittodrie. By this time teenage Rangers fans were taking victories over our two fiercest foes as almost run-of-the-mill. For guys like me, who went through puberty as Rangers went through the worst period in their history, these wins will never be taken for granted.

There's also another generation that may not quite regard the Souness revolution as dearly as myself. Rangers fans in their fifties and older who remember the days of Jim Baxter in his pomp or maybe even the 'Iron Curtain' defence of George Young and co. But the earliest Rangers memory I have is my aunt and uncle taking me to Ibrox for the first time, as a seven-year-old, in April 1977, as we beat Hibs in front of 10,000. A Scottish Cup final defeat to Celtic awaited but this was the season between the two trebles, between the second and third championships we'd win 'in colour'. It'd be a long wait till the fourth and, as much as I revere the team of John Greig, Sandy Jardine and co, they were always vulnerable to an Aberdeen or Celtic side over the course of a season – and virtually anybody in the top flight on any given day.

What Souness did was to make the rearguard so solid it could defend with ferocity whenever required and the attack so potent it could provide the goals we needed against whatever obstacle was put in front of it. In the heart of these two forces, linking it all, beat a patient but simmering tempo, best imparted by Souness himself but soon delegated to Durrant, McMinn, Cooper and even Cammy Fraser. The new credo went, 'When it's not happening, don't panic and don't concede. When it is happening, attack and kill.' The high ball up to the centre forward was dead – long live the grounded passing game. Adding Chris Woods and Terry Butcher to your defence and Souness himself to the midfield were all sure-fire guarantees of silverware. Colin West up front was *not* the solution. This £200,000, 23-year-old from Watford FC was Souness's first Rangers signing, his attempt to buy a purely 'promising' player. When West succumbed to injury and his own lack of talent, Souness decided he was much better off following his primal transfer market instinct – spending a lot on proven quality. Behaving like a canny, thrifty manager just did not suit.

West might have been his first player signing but his first personnel recruitment of any kind was perhaps the best signing Souness ever made and one that would bring Rangers untold glory long after Souness himself had departed Glasgow. Walter Smith – assistant manager at Dundee United, and to the Scotland national team during the 1986 World Cup finals – was the man with his finger on the pulse of the Scottish domestic scene. For years under the aegis of Jim McLean at Tannadice, Smith had no problems remaining number two if it could be at the club he'd adored as a kid.

A man who cut as measured and modest a public figure as Souness appeared glamorous and confrontational, Smith was a quietly hard man. His calm demeanour was wrought from steel. Though no-one would guess it from his on-camera persona, Walter Smith was not averse to inviting training-ground mutineers into the privacy of the dressing room, locking the door and offering them the first punch. Here was the studied personality who had studied the Scottish football scene his entire life. Alex Totten and John Hagart departed Ibrox along with Jock Wallace, and Walter Smith was a change in the right direction in terms of coaching staff. However, mere change was not enough to retrieve Rangers from the embarrassment they'd become to the heavyweights of British football they'd soon be; what was required was a tectonic shift. That could only manifest itself through a singularly chaotic, destructive force of nature. Smith was, if you like, the method behind the Souness madness.

Despite the distorted view from the present day, the signings in Souness's first year in charge were not as many or always as ostentatious as we think. And although a good number of players did leave in the summer of 1986, the clear-out was not as brutal, comprehensive or instantaneous as we imagine. Veteran striker/centre half Derek Johnstone, young reserve goalie Andy Bruce, red-haired stopper Dave McKinnon and flat-faced midfielder Billy Davies were the main frees. Souness brought Jimmy Nichol back for a second spell, in exchange for Bobby Williamson to West Brom, early in the new season. A lot of the players from Wallace's reign were retained and rejuvenated.

Apart from the stadium, over the last five or so years Davie Cooper was the only other reminder that Rangers were a great club. The crabbit, brilliant, Rangers through-and-through winger was born ready for the Souness revolution. In the club's wilderness years his loyalty was often deemed myopic. Everyone expected Cooper to flee the sinking Rangers ship for the riches and glamour of the English scene; when Ruud Gullit, making a go of it at a wee outfit called AC Milan, referred to him as the best player he'd ever come up against, we Bears also wondered why Coop was still in Govan. His genius was such that we wouldn't be surprised if he'd actually known all along that the glamour and excitement of the English scene would soon be coming to Glasgow. Souness never had a problem with Cooper, never badgered or harangued him. He had too much respect for a man he saw as possessing a talent as world class as his own.

Ally Dawson stayed although Ted McMinn lasted until his

indiscipline saw him sold back to Jock Wallace at Seville in 1987. Cammy Fraser – a man who once celebrated a Bad Old Days goal against St Mirren by shoving two fingers in the direction of the Govan stand – was a mainstay in the midfield for much of Souness's first full season until injury forced his premature retirement from the game. Craig Paterson was allowed to hang around the fringes for a few months and make the odd first-team appearance. Dave McPherson played in all but two of the league games in 1986/87, either at right back or in central defence. McCoist set a new post-war league scoring record, Durrant was at the heart of everything, including scoring the winner in the first Souness league meeting with Celtic. This was not an Abramovich-style takeover where a whole new team was planted on us overnight.

Graham Roberts came in to seal things up. We were actually nine points off the top in November. But Souness wasn't about to have his 'rebuilding' season. He wasn't waiting that long and, luckily, he had a chairman who was as impatient as himself: David Holmes helped him buy Tottenham and England centre half Roberts – a very hard man who'd attended October's Skol Cup final with Chris Waddle and described it as the best atmosphere he had ever experienced. His debut against Dundee United saw him put a two-footed tackle into a United player out on the east enclosure touchline. Who it was I don't recall; Paul Sturrock perhaps, maybe Kevin Gallacher? For me it was one of those faceless, tippy-tappy, *speed-meisters* in tangerine and black who'd helped United scale the heights of the premier division and Europe for the last few years while Rangers plumbed the depths of the Anglo-Scottish Cup against Chesterfield. Whoever it was, Roberts brutalised him. It should have been a sending off. It wasn't, so he stayed on the field to give another offering to the Bears.

Later, as he pushed up to help our attack, he found himself tackling opposing defenders as they tried to clear. He was soon turning a 40–60 with United keeper Billy Thomson into a body-crunching challenge that spun the ball out for Robert Fleck to slot into an empty net. We won 2–0 and Roberts had done it his way – which was our way.

No games were easy; everyone could beat everyone in those days. And there were no guaranteed sell-outs every week. Anything over 20,000 was a big crowd in the mid-eighties for Rangers and 38,000 was a real turn up. And beating Motherwell 1–0, especially after they'd reversed that score on us on their first visit to Ibrox, was a seminal result. Today it's 3–0 against Livingston, Motherwell, Dunfermline and everyone else except Celtic and it's 50,000 at every home game, no matter the opponents. This modern luxury, about which the majority of the current Rangers support is so apathetic, was earned by the grit and determination of the Souness forebears. These, my young friends, were the war years.

Can't remember what Dingy was wearing but Ronnie and I definitely had the crew-neck jerseys Rangers had been sporting for the last two seasons. This season we'd ditched the red and black socks of tradition and replaced them with pure red socks – they made the strip appear lighter, although it retained its essential Union Jack look. It went well with jeans, that top, but in the heat of an August sun bouncing its rays off the tenements and tarmac of Easter Road's long incline away from the ground, we wished we had the shorts on too. I had 'Cooper' and a number 11 on the back of my jersey – printed by Roes sports shop in Chapelwell Street, Saltcoats – but Ronnie hadn't dived in so quick to have his back printed with the one good player we had during the dark days of our worst-ever season. He waited till the summer and went for 'Souness' and that old half-back number. The wide Edinburgh thoroughfare wasn't silent but, more eerily, packed with visiting bodies making relatively little noise – until one older voice, from amidst the beaten figures behind, shouted 'Ho! Number 4! Yer aff!'

Walter Smith's faultlessly diplomatic, secretary-manager style was a return to the halcyon, mythical days of Struth and Symon – the level of domestic dominance exceeded even anything Rangers had achieved either side of the second world war – but none of it would have been possible without Souness's utterly abrasive, deliberately embattled style. What he was as a player he could never bring in full to the Scottish domestic scene. He claims Caledonia's referees had it in for him. Others would argue (from a distance!) that the prescribed impossibility of mixing management and playing is particularly axiomatic at a club the size of Rangers. Sent-off in both the opening game of his first full premier division season and the day Rangers won their first title under his leadership – with no cause for argument in either case – Souness had clearly become a caricature of himself to some extent when choosing the most direct method of guiding his team. But this was only because, as much as his legs were slowing, his inability to execute his on-field skills as he once did resulted in that very character coming to the fore in every other aspect of his Ibrox remit. In Govan, Souness the player eventually passed away to let Souness the character take over.

But a slowing and distracted Graeme Souness the midfielder was still enough to captain Scotland to a World Cup finals *after* he'd walked up the marble staircase that the portrait of the Wee Blue Devil himself, Alan Morton, presides over. His ability, between red cards, to control so many Rangers matches like an on-field puppeteer – each pass a sumptuous lifting of a string that breathed championship life into the Ibrox marionettes – made as massive a contribution to a few early trophy wins as his first plunges into the transfer market. Having not yet turned thirty-three at the time of Jock Wallace's dismissal, Graeme Souness was, along with his former Liverpool and Scotland teammate Kenny Dalglish, the only Scotsman playing the game who could be truly called world class. To have him dressed in Rangers trousers, blazer, shirt and tie, then full Rangers strip, wasn't so much a wake-up call to every one of those clubs who'd lorded it over us for the past decade as a mortal wounding. As statements of intent go, this was a double-barrel shotgun (probably an ornately decorated Italian hunting rifle), pointed at head-height.

Lawrence Marlborough was the man seizing control of Rangers in the build-up to Souness's arrival. The American-based business-man installed Falkirk-born David Holmes as Ibrox chief executive, later chairman, to unlock the audience, spending and football potential that had all but evaporated from G51 since the glorious treble of 1978. Holmes engineered the situation in which Scottish football's most mercenary figure would surrender a life in Italy and Serie A, where British football's most fearsome competitor of the day would ditch the chance of another couple of seasons playing against the likes of Zico and Maradona, so he could play alongside the likes of Stuart Munro and Ted McMinn.

The man who infamously said 'I play football for money – I am a football mercenary' was suddenly wearing the Rangers blazer and talking about the Govan club as the biggest in Great Britain – through misguided affection rather than calculating mind game. But Marlborough and Holmes were gone from Rangers within a couple of years, that same mercenary fixation tempting them to sell Scotland's biggest club to a young man who couldn't get on the board at Ayr United. Souness stayed on. Some people, particularly in the press, forget that Graeme Souness smoothed the way for mil-lionaire businessman David Murray to arrive at Ibrox and not vice versa. When Murray did arrive at Ibrox, on 23 November 1988, his friend had been manager for two-and-a-half years. Rangers cost their most explosive managerial appointment a marriage and almost certainly sowed the seeds of his early nineties coronary trouble. For once in his life Graeme Souness was giving more to football than it was giving him back – and the payee was Rangers FC.

We played football with Gerry and Franny doon the Glebe quite a lot. They were always playing football. Gerry, under just as many different aliases, was in about three different amateur/Sunday league teams. As we walked across that self-same expanse of council grass, under the shadow of the highest buildings in Saltcoats, the two brothers, engulfed in their regulation hoops, stopped knocking the ball back and forward and came over

to talk to us. No slaggings here. We were stood in our Rangers jerseys and
everyone knew everyone else's results. The brothers just wanted to know
how it had happened. We told them about the sending-off, the rammy, the
twenty-one bookings, the surplus crowd lifting the exit gate off its hinges
at kick-off. They told us about Celtic Park – probably with more like
90,000 in it – as the championship flag went up against Dundee. We'd
probably bump into them in town that night if we could be bothered try-
ing to get in for a beer somewhere.

Within the axis on which Rangers turned the corner into the
modern footballing age, the Edinburgh-born Spurs, Middlesbrough,
Liverpool, Sampdoria and Scotland midfielder was the main constant.
Walter Smith's smooth style in the hot seat, his polishing of an
already well-oiled machine, would've been of no use to Rangers in
1986. We hadn't won the league in nine long seasons, were actually
struggling to qualify for even the least of Europe's competitions
when Souness was appointed and had, in fact, only been champions
of Scotland three times in the two decades since the notorious
dismissal of Scot Symon . . . which took place when Graeme Souness
was fourteen years old.

Symon was everything except officially sacked in November
1967, with Rangers top of the league and having already defeated
European champions Celtic in that same league campaign. But the
calamitous cup defeat to lowly Berwick Rangers helped darken the
shadow cast by Celtic's triumph in Lisbon. Then chairman John
Lawrence sacked a manager who'd won six league championships,
five Scottish Cups, four League Cups and guided Rangers to two
European finals. David Holmes – appointed to the John Lawrence
organisation by the same man – was himself chairman when Souness
managed Rangers to their next worst Scottish Cup defeat, against
Hamilton Academicals exactly twenty years later. Holmes learned
the mistake of his mentor, didn't even consider sacking Souness or
his strikers – Robert Fleck and Ally McCoist were as responsible
for the 1–0 loss to Accies in the eyes of older fans as Jim Forrest and

George McLean were culpable just south of the border in 1967 – and stuck with his appointment to the manager's post. The following week Souness, McCoist and Fleck all scored as Rangers destroyed Hearts' eighteen-month unbeaten home record with a 5–2 win at Tynecastle. Rangers won that season's league championship and in the next four years Souness added another three. When he left in April 1991 Rangers were a month away from their fourth title in five seasons.

The two cup defeats that have humiliated Rangers more than any others in our thirteen-decade history now sit like bookends at each extreme of the leanest period in this fine club's existence. Jock Wallace won three league titles and two trebles in the space of four mid-seventies seasons but for eleven years before and for the nine years subsequent Rangers were without a single championship to their famous name.

You can only go from this set of circumstances to the almost undiluted success which followed Rangers for the fourteen years after 1986 if a very special force of nature is employed to do the job. Souness was described by Tommy Docherty as a man so hard he could watch an entire episode of *Little House on the Prairie* without shedding a tear. When Liverpool playwright Alan Bleasdale wanted the epitome of glamorous steel to juxtapose with Yosser Hughes's psychotic street tough in the BBC drama *Boys from the Blackstuff*, he cast Graeme Souness. In the episode of *Eastenders* where the Queen Vic bar staff face Wilmot Brown's wine-bar staff across a five-a-side pitch, Dirty Den sidles up to Lofty before kick-off and snarlingly asks if his traitorous former employee knows the identity of the Walford villain's footballing hero. Tom Watts's character quivers 'erm, no' and Lesley Grantham stretches to new depths of soap-baddie menace when he moves to within biting distance and growls that most growlable Christian name before hissing that most hissable surname, 'Grrrrayum Ssssooooooness'.

A synonym for 'hard man'? No. It was more than that. Souness was darker than just your run-of-the-mill tough-nut or hatchet man; he was, when needs be, vicious. My father used to follow Scotland; from the sixties up till the nineties he'd be at most matches at Hampden and there were a good few trips to Wembley thrown in. But when I once quizzed him about the worst tackle he'd ever seen, he surprised me by naming a match I'd attended with him. 'Souness against Peter Nicholas at Hampden'. This challenge had caught not just my dad's eye, but that of the Welsh international midfielder too; right in the cornea. Head-high 'tackles' were thought to be the stuff of those temperamental Latin types – until Graeme Souness took a dislike to you. As Frank Worthington once confessed to a tabloid, 'If I had to nominate the hardest, most ruthless player I've come up against in fifteen years of top class football, I would give the dubious award to [then] Liverpool captain Graeme Souness . . . he isn't just hard, there's definitely a nasty side to him.'

Rangers, as a football club, were always considered 'hard', in the days anything from Glasgow was deemed mean by Britain-at-large. But we had that nasty side too. Rangers were the club that very obviously didn't sign Catholics and mostly never admitted it. Well, now we were the club which had a 45,000-capacity, mostly seated, fully-roofed, stadium – one of the best in Europe – and didn't have a team capable of filling it. Souness and Rangers was a match made in both heaven and hell – the former is where we ended up but the latter was where he found us languishing. Hell is where the man himself and some of his signings seemed to have learned their craft.

I've seen footage of an Ipswich–Liverpool clash from the early eighties and it is Graeme Souness squatting in the middle of the Portman Road pitch as the referee awards a free kick. Our future manager grimaces in agony, catching his breath and checking all the parts are still there. The Liverpool captain has been hurt but he's in no hurry to seek retribution. The camera then closes in on a man mountain in East Anglian blue, running back to organise his defence with a look of 'That'll teach that bastard' etched across his knotted face. Terry Butcher was intended to go to Tottenham or Manchester United when Ipswich hit hard times; Souness brought him to Rangers for £725,000.

Butcher's first tackle in Rangers colours came against Dieter Hoeness of Bayern Munich in a pre-season friendly. The sun shone, Hoeness received the ball with his back to the Copland Road goal and Butcher took the ball then the giant German in one gloriously legal assault which took the roof off the Brox. The following May, his hair newly shorn, he'd rise above the Miller–McLeish central defence to power home our only goal on the day he won his first championship. In between times he let nothing past and caused mayhem in opposition boxes at set-pieces.

By late December Rangers weren't as far up the league as their investment in Butcher, England goalie Chris Woods (£600,000 from Norwich City) and Souness himself (£300,000 to the Genovese) merited. So Graham Roberts was snapped up from Spurs for £450,000 – one year after his new manager wrote in his autobiography, 'I am certainly not as hard as [Kenny Burns] or the Spurs centre back Graham Roberts who is as tough a player as I have come across in recent years'. In deciding who he wanted in his dressing room, Souness went for the only players he could think of who actually scared him. He wasn't interested in individuals he knew he could boss around; he wanted the kind of men who would boss around the whole of Scottish football.

It was New Year's Day, it was snowing a drizzly blizzard and we were a wee bit hungover. 17 years had been old enough for our first ever post-bells freedom. Our tickets were for up the back of the main stand – the very back row, the very first three seats, tucked right up in the corner at the Copland Road side. The way the old main stand roof overhung, we could only see the pitch and the first few rows of the other three stands. The talk had been as much about the game as the drunken out-of-hand badness I'd been up to in the wee-small hours and the set of Celtic fans we'd just about square-goed in the concourse. (Why did we still give them so much of our ground?) But we were miffed that we wouldn't be able to see all the punters here today. That's what an Old Firm game is about – the atmosphere. Then again we hadn't thought about Roy Aitken marking Souness. Davie Hay obviously wanted Celtic's hard man to get after his international teammate and shut him down. After five minutes Souness let the ball come off his foot by about ten yards – a really bad touch. At least, that's how he wanted it to appear. . . . As Aitken scurried out to the wing to collect it, our manager went into him from the back. Aitken just about ended up in the west enclosure, alongside all the soaking-wet Celtic fans. Souness took a yellow card, we scored two goals before half time and Ronnie got up onto his wooden seat faster than me each time so when he grabbed me to celebrate my specs got squashed all over my face, via his jacket. Then Souness stood on the ball in the middle of the park. He lifted his kicking leg one way and three Celtic players went left. He lifted it another way and they went right. He motioned to smack it down the middle and they all stood still. At no point did he actually move the ball and at no point could anyone see Roy Aitken anywhere near the action. He was all on his own, Souness. No-one would give him a game. We went ballistic. Ibrox howled adoration and domination. All the way home on the bus we listened to Celtic fans on the phone-ins claiming the captain of the reigning champions was a coward.

This was something that couldn't be said of the Rangers my gran bemoaned during my 'Clearasil' years. 'I remember when Rangers won the league all the time' she told me one Sunday afternoon in the early eighties as I visited her in typically grief-stricken teenage mode. Other lads and lassies at school used Joy Division or The Smiths as conduits for their existential angst. But I wasn't worried about why Ian Curtis hung himself and the happiest, most joyous concert I ever attended was Morrisey and Johnny Marr giving it laldy at the Magnum arena in Irvine in 1985. Music was fun dammit. For me there were very real, very immediate reasons to be depressed. The *Encyclopaedia of World Football* on my bookcase told me in greater detail how Rangers dominated those black-and-white days. I had fading post-potty-training memories of Jock

Wallace running onto pitches to molest John Greig's hair in the early colour days. But Rangers were being left well behind at the dawn of my modern age.

Celtic's nine-in-a-row also screamed at me from that same *Encyclopaedia*. No matter how hard I looked, from Albania to Yugoslavia, from Algeria to Zaire, no other legitimate nine-in-a-row could be found in any other domestic set-up on the planet. If Rangers couldn't ever do it then I would damn well cheer on the Stasi-sponsored Dynamo Berlin as they tortured, bribed and intimidated their way towards ten-in-a-row in East Germany. Celtic's *NIAR* was barely a decade old so it hung over me more darkly every time they topped it up with a wee singular title triumph like 1977 or '79, or another wee two-in-a-row like 1981 and '82. Parenthesising this we had the insolent, salt-in-the-wound championship triumphs of Aberdeen and Dundee United. I was barely able to cope with the one-sidedness of the Old Firm rivalry, now we had the New Firm pissing all over us too. Heaven knew I was miserable now – but then this charming man came along and we weren't just breaking our own championship duck, we were bringing back the monarchical domination my gran knew of and replanting it in the modern era.

And if we hadn't struck when we did, we'd not have caught onto the football boom the way we did. The way I heard the news of Souness's arrival was what made it great; you knew everyone else in the country was watching the evening news with you. But it was also a startling contrast to the SMS text, internet, 24-hour-football-satellite-channel world we live in now. Rangers moved into their latest phase of power just in time to catch the most modern age of communication. Their successes were massive from the Souness signing onwards and the relaying of news of those successes became increasingly advanced. The whole of Italy already knew about the Sampdoria star who had knocked back another season in Serie A for this club called Rangers. England was forced to watch as its best centre half and most promising goalie went north. And the onset of global, instantaneous communication would ensure every other corner of the planet could receive information about Rangers and their spending.

Long after Souness was an Ibrox memory, the club he left behind would sign Paul Gascoigne, Brian Laudrup and a Chilean, a Brazilian, an Argentinean, the captain of the United States soccer team. The brand name was there, the methods of selling it were arriving; all Rangers had to do in 1986 was ensure it had a team capable of maintaining the brand's reputation. Souness was the explosion that propelled us from history books to the mobile phones of football fans, agents and players in every continent. We couldn't regurgitate Alan Morton, George Young or even Jim Baxter's heyday simply to re-sell 'Rangers FC' through new media. Even the Cup Winners' Cup triumph in Barcelona in 1972 managed to catch the tail-end of football broadcasting in black and white. Our previous successes were monochrome; colour television only recorded our darkest days. So we didn't regurgitate the past, we matched it – we exceeded it. If Terry Butcher and Graeme Roberts aren't a colour version of George Young and Willie Woodburn then I don't know what is. Cooper to McCoist was a 'Waddell and a Noddle' and the yellow jersey with the yellow hair and the movie star looks, Chris Woods, was Bobby Brown all over again. By the time you could have colour television footage e-mailed to you on your thumb-sized mobile phone, Rangers were at the forefront of British footballing might.

Everything that instigated this climb to the corporate, cynical centre of things contrived in a sea of unexpected sincerity back in 1985 to 1986: Souness was the symbol of Scottish football able to compete on the European stage. He had in his power that which our fans and our media coveted most: the ability to win. Not only were his talents supreme, but unlike so many past greats of the Scottish game, his off-field behaviour and career choices were unfalteringly correct. He was the best midfielder in the English game and he had three European Cup winner's medals to prove it. He'd gone to Italy and brought Sampdoria their first ever domestic honour. He led his country in two World Cup tournaments after enjoying a side-role in his first. Apart from the usual naughty-boy stuff in his late teens and early twenties his private life was settled and his commitment to physical fitness almost legendary. He'd earned the highest respect in the domestic game, reached the zenith of achievements with Liverpool and he'd maintained his health to the stage where he could test himself in the world's most arduous league while raking in a small fortune and lapping up the Italian lifestyle. He was a player in every sense.

This appointment showed the Rangers support, the rest of Scotland, the rest of the football planet, in one fell swoop, that Rangers were no longer 'playing at it'. Yet – most crucially – for a man who'd never spent a second in a Rangers jersey, Souness had an instant affinity in the eyes of Beardom; his style of play was the realist, pragmatic opposite of the sentimental, 'jinky' pile of mawkishness that emanated from Celtic Park. But, more than that, he had actually declared on film, a year earlier, at a time when the boardroom set-up at Rangers meant he could never be approached that he would one day love to become player-manager of Rangers. This, of course, was the board that forced the very average Northern Ireland centre half John McLelland out of the captaincy and Scotland because it wouldn't break the almost Victorian pay structure.

Put together in September 1985, the legendary BBC television documentary *Only A Game?* – from which the even more legendary spoof *Only An Excuse* took its name – focused on the Scottish fixation with the national team. Graeme Souness was interviewed in Cardiff, probably on the eve of that World Cup qualifier against Wales overshadowed by the passing of the great Jock Stein. To hear a man like this – a man who, despite his Scottish roots, seemed as distant from the world of the premier league and four-figure crowds at Ibrox as Deacon Blue were from the Rolling Stones – even acknowledging that Rangers existed was a thrill. The man of the cold, hard stare turned away with an embarrassed grin, almost giggling bashfully like some schoolgirl confessing a crush for a member of a boy band. He did actually say the words, albeit in self-deprecating sarcasm, 'Jock Wallace watch out'. The fact that it came amid a statement of Souness's complete lack of affection for anything other than money and success – with Rangers being the caveat! – stood the mousta-chioed one in great stead when he did come through those doors at Edmiston Drive. Everyone and their dog declared how lovely it would be to play for those amazingly sporting and jocular Celtic fans – without ever doing it. We had the one guy on the planet without pity or sentiment . . . and he actually liked us. We were his weakness.

Even in succumbing to this private Ibrox fixation, he still had to try and overcome us, dominate the Rangers beast. He told us he would sign a Catholic; he did. He told us he just saw the Old Firm derbies as another two points; we changed his mind on that one. Souness and the Rangers support scored one each: it was a fight even while it was a love affair and both parties had a tacit under-standing of why. Explosiveness, chaos, a perpetual state of flux: this is how our new manager lived and got things done. He reduced the entire panorama of Scottish football to the one thing he understood: a midfield melee.

It was the late mid-eighties and Graeme Souness would even-tually show Margaret Thatcher around Ibrox. The *Daily Records* of the world loved it but so did Souness. Thatcher was a borderline psychotic who always dressed smart for the executions she'd organised. Souness was never seen out of an Armani suit, if he wasn't in a Rangers blazer. The two most infamous mercenaries known to the Scottish people were glad, almost proud, to be in each other's company. Souness was daring anyone to have a problem with it; confrontations were what he knew. Causing mayhem caused success. This lady's not for turning and neither is this laddie – no-one likes us, we don't care.

The day his name first appeared in a football programme as our boss – Saturday, 12 April 1986 – we lost to lowly Clydebank at Kilbowie. When he took his first bow in front of the Gers support we qualified for Europe on the last day of the league season by beating Motherwell 2–0. But, a five minute drive down the M8, Celtic were winning the most unexpected championship in their history; six days later Souness's first Old Firm game as manager involved a packed Ibrox shoving Celtic's celebrations down their throat with a 3–2 Glasgow Cup final victory.

Souness's competitive debut as a player ended with him red-carded for inflicting a four-inch gash on George McCluskey's shin – the very one that helped poke home the winner in the 1980 Old Firm Scottish Cup final – as the former Celt tried to act the hard man. Souness was letting the Premier Division know he'd take no prisoners . . . we lost 2–1 at Hibs in the opening league fixture of the 86/87 season and the world seemed to collapse. A symbolic home win over Aberdeen was capped with a Souness goal of revenge against the manager who had dropped him from the Scotland team during that summer's World Cup finals and a Robert Fleck winner caused Jim Leighton to sprint halfway down the pitch to get at the linesman who'd allowed it. The pivotal Ne'erday victory over Celtic at Ibrox, with Souness playing his finest game in a Rangers jersey and matching Baxter in his arrogant domination, was enshrouded by sleet and snow and the pitch covered in muck and Souness took a yellow as he kicked Roy Aitken into the west enclosure in the opening exchanges. On the night we went out of Europe to Borussia Mönchengladbach on away goals, in the third round of the UEFA Cup, we played the Germans off the pitch in the Boekelberg, hitting the bar and having both Davie Cooper and Stuart Munro sent off. We went top of the league in January for the first time in nine years with a 2–0 home win over Hamilton Accies – red cards were shown, Terry Butcher clattered goalies, balls were bundled over lines, snow, damp and dark again framed the stadium. When Souness won his first major domestic honour, the League Cup, we defeated Celtic 2–1 at Hampden in a final that included Maurice Johnston 'blessing' himself in front of the Rangers fans as he was sent off and Celtic's Shepherd being red-carded for hitting the referee, then allowed back onto the pitch when the ref realised he'd actually been hit by a coin from the crowd and then . . . then . . .

We go to Pittodrie on 2 May 1987 knowing a win at a stadium we just didn't win at was necessary to secure the title. Rangers fans took over at least half the ground. Souness was having trouble containing the home side's young midfielder Brian Irvine so he crudely tried to put him out of the game and was sent off. Irvine scored at the end of the first half but Terry Butcher had already converted a Davie Cooper free-kick shortly after we'd gone down to ten men. It finished 1–1 but Celtic lost at home to Falkirk and we were the champions and our fans invaded the pitch and, well, it was chaos.

Hell, we didn't know the polis let the Gers fans without tickets into Pittodrie after the final whistle to join in the celebrations. Anytime we'd been to Aberdeen before, the Grampian polis had been absolute bastards. We didn't know that the money we ended up spending on champagne could have bought us a wee tranny and that we could have listened to the game outside Pittodrie and then got in as the final whistle blew. That stuff all came out in the days after. But I did know one thing. Even at seventeen years old, one thing myself, Ronnie and Dingy, out of all the under-age regulars crowded round that speaker in the Stanley hotel knew best, as we looked over the beautiful Firth of Clyde towards scenic Arran and tried to envisage a miserable wee patch of grass in Aberdeen, was that this championship win would mean more to us than any other Rangers would ever secure.

Think it was the moment Richard Park or whoever the hell did the commentaries in those days said 'Rangers are the champions' that had me bubbling first. A night on the tiles on the Costa Del Saltcoats and Ardrossan ended prematurely as we were chucked out the Celtic-sympathetic Laurieston bar for reciprocating David Holmes's on-screen toast and cheering

Big Tel's header. Why the hell did they have Sportscene on anyway? An understanding father allowed me to sit snivelling to myself as I watched the highlights on video later that night. He didn't mention the steamingness – but, then again, I had punishment enough waiting round the corner. Before anyone else could tell me in more callous tones, my mother and father gently cornered me in my room the following Monday night. They told me what my uncle had witnessed at that supporters' club meeting I missed: my name coming out the hat.

If you're not at the meeting then you can't get your ticket; no-one can pick it up for you. That was a sore one. Even I took a kicking when Souness arrived.

But, then again, if you weren't at Ibrox when 10,000 endured a draw with Morton or Clydebank in the middle of a season that was already lost, in the middle of an era that was free of championship titles and full of ridicule by press and rivals, then you don't know exactly how lucky you are to be supporting Rangers today. I feel pretty darned lucky.

There have been more exciting championship wins since: beating Aberdeen on the last day of the 90/91 season, overtaking Celtic with barely two minutes remaining of the 2004/05 season. There have been more prestigious championship wins: our ninth on the trot in 96/97, securing the 98/99 title at Parkhead. But there has never been a more significant Rangers championship win in my lifetime, and possibly in the second half of the twentieth century, than that of 1986/87. Many people made it possible but they all revolved around one figure. Whether employing him, or employed by him, Graeme Souness is the man they named the revolution after. Graeme Souness was dynamite.

Author's note: The Souness autobiography is *No Half Measures* Graeme Souness with Bob Harris (Grafton Books, 1987).

8

'AND ANYWAY, I DON'T WANT TO GO TO IBROX'

Colin Armstrong

The dying seconds of yet another tense Old Firm league game at Ibrox on 4 November 1989 and the deadlock has yet to be broken. But there is to be one final, dramatic twist. Scottish international striker Maurice Johnston, with over fifty goals for Celtic on his impressive curriculum vitae, picks up a loose clearance at the edge of the Copland Road penalty area and wastes no time as he drills a powerful, right-foot drive low into the corner of the net. Bedlam. Hysteria. Madness. The usual emotions ensue; but this time it's so, so different. For Johnston is wearing light blue – and he has scored a fairytale winner for Rangers against his former club.

Teammate Ally McCoist later jokes that he had to race down Paisley Road West to Cessnock underground station to catch Johnston. But, in reality, the former Celtic star, in a state of unbridled euphoria, dives into the crowd behind the goal where he is mobbed by equally ecstatic Gers fans, many of whom used to despise him. His conversion and acceptance are now all but complete.

In the London studios of BBC Television the normally unflappable sports anchorman Des Lynam tells the nation that Celtic have taken the lead before quickly rectifying his mistake. He informs the puzzled viewers that Johnston has indeed scored – but against his old club in the most dramatic of climaxes. But it was not the most dramatic of days. That had come months earlier, on 10 July 1989, when MoJo became the first leading Catholic player to sign for the Ibrox club in modern times. And it was a day no football fan in Scotland will forget.

There have been many 'where were you?' moments over the years. The murder of President John F. Kennedy in Dallas in 1963 is the original of the genre; the death of Diana, Princess of Wales and the terrorist attacks on the Twin Towers are other examples of incidents that people instantly recall where they were when they heard the news. It is crass to compare football issues in a country of around five million people with events of such global significance, but there is little doubt that everyone with even just a passing interest in Scottish football remembers where they were on the day that Maurice Johnston signed for Rangers. I had just left school and had been wakened by my dad who told me that there was to be a 'big announcement' at Ibrox at ten that morning. I listened to the Radio Clyde bulletin that broke the news and, like most people, I could hardly believe it.

In modern times only Alfie Conn had crossed the great divide and played for both clubs; first for the Gers before returning to Scotland after a spell with Spurs to play for Celtic. That had been newsworthy, but the fact that Johnston was the first high-profile Catholic to play for Rangers in decades added more spice to an already explosive announcement. The icing on the cake, however, was the fact that MoJo had seemed destined to return to Parkhead just weeks before he arrived in Govan. Indeed, Celtic's victory in the 1989 Old Firm Scottish Cup final arguably had as much to do with Johnston announcing his return than it had to do with the Parkhead side's performance on that sunny afternoon at Hampden. Rangers, dominant under Graeme Souness, had secured both the League and the League Cup and were going for a glorious treble.

But Celtic were visibly buoyed by the prospect of Johnston's return and they owed as much to their former striker's presence in the stand for the 1–0 victory as they did to Joe Miller for his match-winning strike.

Ironically, though, the deal to bring him to Rangers was on its way to completion by time the final was played, if legend is to be believed. One story goes that Souness stormed into the dressing room after the game and hurled his loser's medal across the floor. He then, it is said, made a comment that no one really understood. It went along the lines of: 'don't worry lads, there will be something happening very soon that will wipe the smiles off their faces'. No one asked what Souness was referring to, but it seems entirely possible that Johnston was celebrating in the winners' dressing room with his new teammates – knowing that he was going to be a Rangers player the following season.

Johnston, though, had courted controversy long before he decided to move to Rangers. He had started his career at Partick Thistle, before moving to Watford where he made an FA Cup final appearance against Everton in 1984. He then moved to the club he had supported as a boy, Celtic, and it was in this period that he started to appear as much on the front pages as on the back. Trouble was never far away. He made several court appearances to explain a variety of misdemeanours – from resetting tracksuits to assault – and his tangled love life provided good copy for the tabloids.

The degree of controversy that surrounded him also led to a fair amount of urban myth. That he was the only Celtic player to wear a long-sleeve jersey was deemed worthy of scurrilous – and untrue – rumours in the pubs and clubs in Glasgow. Some said that the extra fabric was concealing an IRA tattoo, others that it was hiding the many needle marks on his arms. While these were malicious falsehoods, one thing, however, was a cast-iron certainty: Johnston's relationship with the Rangers fans. He didn't like us; we didn't think too much of him. And both parties liked it that way.

The root cause of the animosity towards Johnston by the Rangers support was due primarily to his open disdain for the Ibrox club. He was also never far away from any controversy in Old Firm games, something that made him a cult hero with the Celtic support. A friend who frequents Parkhead once told me that Johnston got far more adulation from the Hoops support than strike partner Brian McClair could have ever wished for – despite the fact that the latter had the healthier goals tally. But McClair didn't represent the Celtic support in the same way as Johnston did; he was one of them, a man who was not afraid to show his true colours or talk about how much he disliked Celtic's biggest rivals. In his autobiography, *Mo: The Maurice Johnston Story*, Johnston states:

> Let me just spell out where I stand here. I'm a Celtic man through and through and so dislike Rangers because they are a force in Scottish football and a threat to the club I love. But more than that I hate the religious policy which they maintain. Why won't they sign a Roman Catholic? I hate religious bigotry and Rangers fans always tried to single me out in Old Firm games.

This, of course, told only half the story. As a Celtic player, Johnston was only too willing to court controversy in Old Firm games. Once, on scoring a goal against Rangers at Ibrox, he ran to the delirious Broomloan Road stand where the visiting fans were housed and 'blessed' himself. This was something he repeated in the Skol Cup final at Hampden on being shown the red card for head-butting Gers defender Stuart Munro. It was the latter incident that cemented Johnston's place as a symbol of hate for the Rangers support. The attack on Munro was bad enough but the misplaced religious gesture was seen as a deliberate attempt to wind up the Rangers support. Such a gesture should not, admittedly, provoke outrage in normal circumstances. But there is considerable religious tension in Glasgow between the two major communities. In addition, it is a fact that this particular player rarely, if ever, spent his Sunday mornings at mass; quite clearly his gestures were a deliberate attempt to provoke the kind of response it got. MoJo was daft; but he wasn't stupid.

Nevertheless, by the 1980s, the Ibrox club's anti-Catholic signing policy had become a problem and Johnston was not the only one asking questions. Rangers had signed Catholic teenager John Spencer, who was playing in the youth side, but it had not stopped the criticism. That would change, albeit slowly, with the arrival of Graeme Souness. The former Liverpool star had replaced Jock Wallace in the spring of 1986 and made it clear from the start that he would not shy away from signing the players he needed to do the job – regardless of their religion. He would stick to his word. Souness apparently tried to sign Catholics such as Ray Houghton, a Castlemilk-born Republic of Ireland player, as well as Englishman Paul Bernard, but both refused. It was not going to be easy finding a Catholic to be a pioneer; which made the arrival of Johnston all the more sensational.

There are many stories in circulation as to how the signing came about. The official explanation at the time was that Souness acted after hearing that Celtic's move to sign him had broken down. But rumour, inconsistencies and a revamping of the official version of events suggest that this was simply not the case. It is now difficult to believe that Souness just moved in after Celtic had dropped the ball, and it seems more likely that Johnston was approached by Rangers well before he reached the impasse with Celtic. MoJo was first paraded by Celtic on 12 May and, standing next to Celtic boss Billy McNeill, he told the assembled media: 'It's a dream! I never thought they'd want me back. I had offers from the continent and England but I wanted to wear the green and white again. Deep down, I've always wanted to be back at Celtic.'

It was smiles all round but this togetherness wasn't consistent with comments that Johnston had made in his book, in which he complains about McNeill's handling of his transfer from Celtic to Nantes. He claims that, in a meeting to discuss his departure, McNeill accused him of fabricating offers from other clubs and criticised Johnston's habit of wearing tracksuits and sporting an earring. The player was particularly offended by the first accusation and offered proof of other interested parties. The meeting descended into a slanging match and Johnston indicated that he didn't think that McNeill was the kind of boss he would have enjoyed working for. Yet the pair of them seemed to have buried the hatchet by the time that Johnston was unveiled for a second time as a Celtic player. However, there is the inescapable thought that McNeill's presence at Celtic Park in 1989 had a bearing on Johnston's decision to move to Ibrox.

The first sign that all was not well surfaced on 21 May 1989 when Johnston's agent, Bill McMurdo, hinted at 'contractual problems'. Five days later things appeared to have deteriorated further and Johnston was quoted as saying: 'I wanted so badly to go back to Parkhead but the deal I had tied up doesn't seem to be working out. I'm sorry – I'd like to think my transfer to Celtic could still happen.' But it didn't, and four days later Johnston officially terminated the proposed transfer to Celtic. The Parkhead club disputed this move and, on 26 June, they were backed by FIFA who ruled that Johnston was a Celtic player. The player then threatened to go to the European courts to prove he wasn't. By this time, rumours had begun to circulate about Souness stepping in, but Johnston denied it, claiming: 'Certainly I won't go to Rangers, they don't sign Catholics. And anyway, I don't want to go to Ibrox.'

On 1 July, Celtic, realising the futility of trying to press-gang a player into joining the club, officially withdrew their interest. The next day McMurdo was forced to issue another denial concerning the speculation about a move to Rangers: 'It's a complete fabrication. You could run that story for ten years and it wouldn't be true.' In fact, it wouldn't even take ten days to be proved correct.

From an Ibrox perspective, the background to the remarkable signing has changed slightly in recent years. It is now claimed that it was a throwaway remark by Souness to McMurdo – who was attending a game at Ibrox – that got the ball rolling. Souness apparently asked why he hadn't been notified about Johnston's availability; McMurdo's reply was that the player hadn't actually signed anything. The player was unveiled at Celtic Park on 12 May. Records show there was only one game played at Ibrox after that date that such a conversation could have taken place – and that was on the following day, 13 May, against Aberdeen.

This contradicts the version given at the time that Rangers had stepped in *after* the deal with Celtic had broken down. This was peddled in *Graeme Souness: A Manager's Diary*, published just a few months later. In the book, Souness claims that no contact was made with McMurdo until 4 July, something that is hard to believe. Souness even goes as far to suggest in the book that Johnston didn't sign until the morning he was unveiled, which is even harder to believe. If Souness and McMurdo did have that conversation on 13 May, knowing that Celtic hadn't actually signed Johnston, then Souness's actions were much more calculated than the official version would have us believe.

That said, the stories that have come out of Celtic Park about the whole episode are laughable. On that 12 May presentation to the media, Johnston is said to have raised concerns about the fact that he wasn't actually a Celtic player yet. He was allegedly told by then Parkhead chairman Jack McGinn to just 'kid on' he had signed and they would deal with the formalities in the fullness of time. McMurdo was absent from this unveiling, due to the Celtic board's dislike for a man who was open about his love of Rangers.

It was an absence that further muddies the waters because McMurdo's involvement was without doubt the key to the whole deal. But, even to this day, McMurdo is tight-lipped about it. I met him at the Moat House hotel during the Rangers Supporters' Trust dinner in 2005; an event at which he was a speaker. He agreed to talk about his most controversial transfer deal but gave little away. He asked me what I thought of the deal, to which I replied that I thought it had been great for Rangers. He agreed with that. But the minute I mentioned the inconsistencies in Souness's book about approaching McMurdo on 4 July, the conversation ended. 'I wasn't aware he'd said that', was his reply before leaving me standing in the foyer. The message was clear: he wasn't going to reveal anything.

McMurdo gave a fantastic speech on the night and had his audience in stitches with his stories, a couple of which concerned Johnston's move to Ibrox. One thing, however, came out of my brief meeting with McMurdo: as amateurish as Celtic's handling of the situation had been, they had every reason to feel they'd been gazumped by their oldest rivals and the man they dub Agent Orange.

The immediate aftermath of the signing brought out countless stories that back up my argument. Journalist Jim Black, who broke the story in *The Sun*, recalled that the annual sportswriter's dinner for 1989 – which took place a day after the Old Firm Scottish Cup final – was awash with rumours that Johnston would sign for Rangers. Also, the player allegedly made comments to Ally McCoist at a Scotland get-together about how impressed he was by Graeme Souness's house, a comment that puzzled his international striking partner at the time. Subsequently, McCoist was also apparently in the same room as Johnston when Souness called to talk about the deal. Ally, now aware of the impending signing, could do nothing but shake his head in disbelief at what he was hearing. These incidents took place well before the Celtic deal to sign Johnston broke down.

However, regardless of the chronology involved, there is no doubt Souness saw in Johnston the chance to move his club forward while also landing a blow on his closest rivals. If Celtic had landed Johnston it could be argued that Rangers may not have enjoyed as much success as they did in the following years. It can also be argued that the player practically handed four or five championship titles of what would eventually become nine-in-a-row to Rangers just by putting pen to paper. By bagging MoJo, Souness also ensured that the Celtic board were shown up as incompetent and amateurish. They would not recover for a number of years from the humiliation of losing one of their own to their greatest rivals. Allan Laing summed it up perfectly in the *Glasgow Herald* a day after the signing by commenting, 'Yesterday's announcement in the Blue Room at Ibrox served to show that the art of one-upmanship is still alive and well.'

That Johnston's signing caused so much controversy, however, cannot just be put down to the fact that he was a Catholic. It is hard to imagine the same hullabaloo surrounding the likes of Houghton. The reason Johnston was such a controversial signing is down to a number of factors, of which religion is actually the least important. It is interesting to note that the word 'Catholic' never appeared in the official press-release from the club on the day, nor was it mentioned in the seven-minute announcement to the press. By ignoring his religion in any official capacity the club were making it known that his religion wasn't an issue. He was a good player – and that was enough for Graeme Souness and David Murray.

Johnston's defection to the blue corner initially stunned the Parkhead support and had them questioning just who Rangers wouldn't sign in their quest to be top dogs. Indeed, for a few months following the transfer, paranoid Celtic fans were fearful of consistently losing out to this new, inclusive Ibrox club in the transfer market. When Hibs midfielder John Collins became available a year later, the very real possibility again arose that a boyhood Hoops supporter, who would have been a banker for Celtic only a few months previously, could be lost to their bitter rivals. Collins eventually chose Celtic but had been at Ibrox for talks and came very close to doing a deal with Souness. The Parkhead fans feared their club had lost a major part of its pulling power for players they had considered exclusively theirs in the past. For years, Celtic and their supporters had protested at the injustice of Rangers' signing policy. Now it had changed, they were protesting at what they saw was an even greater injustice.

In fairness, they were not the only ones protesting at this change of direction. Some sections of the Rangers support reacted furiously to the news of Johnston's arrival. Outside the ground a handful of supporters burned scarves and tops, and one even laid a wreath at the front door. The general secretary of the Rangers Supporters Association, David Miller, made what looks in hindsight as an astonishing statement:

> I never thought in my wildest dreams that they would sign him. Why sign him above all others? There will be a lot of people handing in their season tickets. I don't want to see a Roman Catholic at Ibrox. They [Rangers] have always stood for one thing and the biggest majority of supporters have been brought up with a true blue Rangers team.

Such comments are, frankly, embarrassing, and Miller did himself, the Supporters Association and the club no favours at all by expressing them.

However, he was not alone in feeling such anguish at the news. Yet, despite such comments and protest, the predicted boycott never materialised. The doom mongers who predicted Ibrox would be half empty were proved spectacularly wrong. In fact, the average attendance rose slightly during Johnston's first season proving that the majority of the supporters were prepared to move with the times. Some still had reservations about the player chosen to end the policy but it was not enough to stop them from following their side. The much predicted sea of returned season tickets turned out to be a drought and as Ibrox secretary Campbell Ogilvie noted in *Rangers: The Definitive History* the club received only one returned season book after Johnston signed.

One supporter I met – while sitting in a bar watching Rangers end their five-year winless hoodoo at Parkhead against Celtic early in 2005 – typified the complexities that abounded then. He told me that he had been so distraught on hearing that Johnston had signed that he had to take a half-day from his work: 'It felt like a family bereavement', he said. On my questioning why such drastic action was necessary he couldn't really give an answer. Was it because Johnston was Catholic? I was assured that was not the case. He then went on to say it had more to do with him head-butting Stuart Munro than anything else. However, when I asked if he would have reacted in the same way if a player like, say, Jim Bett, had committed the same offence against a Rangers player and had then signed on at Ibrox, he replied 'no'. He concluded that it was probably not the fact that Rangers had signed a Catholic that had upset him, but rather that it was *that* Catholic, the one that had so frequently bitten the hand that was now going to rather handsomely feed him.

This is the case with most Rangers fans I have spoken to who disapproved of the recruitment of Johnston. Very few – if any at all – commented on his religion and all were happy with Johnston's contribution in a blue jersey. The issue for most of them was how he had conducted himself while at Celtic: the Stuart Munro incident, the comments made in his book and so forth. There was also a feeling that the player was only moving to Rangers for the money; that he was a football mercenary. That is not to say that his religion was not an issue for a section of the support. The smart supporter, though, could see the Johnston signing for what it was: a great piece of business for Rangers Football Club.

That is certainly how I reacted on hearing the news. I felt that we had signed a great player first and foremost; but, more importantly, we had won the first Old Firm battle of the season without kicking a ball. For years my Celtic-supporting friends had promised that they would not be shy in letting me know about it the day Rangers signed a Catholic. Yet it had now happened and it was me who was seeking them out to give them a right good ribbing; not the other way about as was supposed to be the case. Not that a Catholic signing for Rangers was ever going to be a problem for me in the first place; it did not bother me in the slightest. At thirty-two, I have had more years of supporting a Rangers side that has employed Catholics than the other way around. I was sixteen when Johnston signed and I can't say I had really bought into the whole 'Protestant-only' concept. When Souness arrived I was prepared to go with what he said would be best for the club as he gave me my first experience of winning a championship after years of supporting a club that regularly finished fourth. That, and having moved away from the west of Scotland at a young age, probably made the transition an easier one for me.

Looking back, though, I feel it was a generational thing. My dad was far from chuffed when it was announced but soon changed his mind when Johnston, in his home debut against Spurs in a friendly, was involved in a fracas with Gary Mabbutt. He wanted players that would fight for the blue jersey and Johnston convinced him he could do that within an hour of his home debut. However, the one person in my family who could not accept it was, strangely, my gran. A woman who never attended any games, to my knowledge, simply would not accept Johnston as a good move for the club and stubbornly rejected my pleas for sense in a phone call to her a couple of days after the signing. I couldn't understand why such a lovely old lady – who had Catholic in-laws and grandchildren – would react in such a way. My conclusion is that because she had lived through a time when the club was a symbolic and representative institution of the Protestant population in Glasgow she found it hard to understand how a Catholic could have the best interests of the club and its supporters at heart. She knew that times had changed and attitudes had softened where religion was concerned, and she was a very tolerant old lady, but it seems that she saw Rangers Football Club as the one thing that would remain a Protestant-only institution.

But what of the Celtic fans? For years prior to Johnston's signing, Celtic and their supporters had held onto the moral high ground surrounding the issue of bigotry, conveniently ignoring the treatment of the man that had won them the European Cup, Jock Stein. In the 1970s Celtic's most successful manager was famously refused a place on the Parkhead board because of his religion, rather shamefully being offered a position in the pools office instead. Moreover, the self-proclaimed greatest fans in the world have also conveniently ignored for years the fact that Alfie Conn – the man who made the opposite journey across the great divide in the seventies – has been back to Ibrox on a number of occasions, and been made very welcome every time. Regardless of these salient points though, the finger generally pointed to Govan when the subject of sectarianism cropped up. Rangers were the main culprits, and always would be while they insisted on not signing Catholics.

The signing of Johnston, however, almost immediately knocked the Parkhead club off the moral high ground they had so jealously guarded. If Johnston had split the Rangers support, he could be safe in the knowledge that he done the opposite with the Celtic fans. Mojo had united his former hero-worshippers in hatred, a hatred that has not mellowed even to this day. Even now, some Hoops fans can barely bring themselves to say Johnston's name preferring instead to use the clichéd 'Judas' or the unsavoury *petite merde*.

Those who were at Celtic Park the first time Johnston appeared as a Rangers player will be able to understand the naked hostility the player engendered amongst those who used to sing his praises. Never in my life have I witnessed at first hand such a level of abuse and Johnston deserved a lot of credit for facing such wrath. He missed two gilt-edged chances and his performance was criticised by many but it wasn't all bad: so desperate were the Celtic defence to stop Johnston from scoring that they stuck three men on him at the first Rangers corner, allowing Terry Butcher a free run and header to give the visitors an early lead in a game that would end

1–1. The crowning moment for Johnston, though, was to come in the next Old Firm game at Ibrox when he silenced his doubters in blue and his critics in green with his last-minute winner against the team he had once proclaimed to love.

The whole hornet's nest was given a huge shaking just recently, in 2005, when Johnston was being touted to play in an 'Auld' Firm match for charity at Hampden Park. The idea was that MoJo would play for Celtic in one half and Rangers in the other but it was something that the Parkhead support wasn't prepared to accept. The Celtic Supporters Association threatened to boycott the match and one of its members was quoted as saying:

> There is too much history and baggage that goes with Johnston. He left Celtic in the lurch in 1989 and went off to sign for Rangers. Celtic supporters will always contribute to charity but, in this instance, they will do it in their own way and won't be going to any game to support Johnston.

That no similar reaction was forthcoming from the present-day Rangers Supporters Association – nor by rank and file Gers fans – reflected well on the club and, indirectly, on Souness and Murray.

Johnston performed heroically for Rangers, particularly in his first season, and was a vital member of the squad in the time that he was there. Rangers received two good years from Johnston and then moved him on to Everton for the same £1.5 million fee they paid for him. Good business indeed. A close friend of mine was once in the company of David Murray, Walter Smith and Archie Knox as a guest of the then Aberdeen manager, Alex Smith, after a game between the two clubs at Ibrox. Sitting in an office in the bowels of the grand stadium, my friend couldn't believe that he was sipping from a tin of McEwan's Lager in such esteemed company. During this get-together, Murray started talking about the recently departed Johnston and claimed that the striker had been his best piece of business since he took over the club; citing the fact that they had got what they paid for the player at a time when his form seemed to be dipping. Murray's overall feeling was that Rangers had got two great years and then their money back on Johnston; no one in the room could argue against the sentiment.

He was cocky, arrogant and had a habit of being able to annoy some people by his very presence but there is no doubt in my mind that Maurice Johnston is the most important player in the recent history of Rangers Football Club. His arrival brought to an end a practice that had become an embarrassment and consequently opened the door for the many great Catholic players that have played for the club since 1989. The nerve shown by Souness and Murray in approaching the player was surpassed only by Johnston accepting the invitation. 'He was a brave wee bugger at the time', the Ibrox owner once commented and when you consider the kind of pressure the Rangers striker was facing then that is a bit of an understatement. Slogans like 'collaborators can't play without kneecaps' – which appeared on a Glasgow wall not long after he signed – were mostly bravado, but that didn't mean that Johnston didn't face a real threat to his well-being by signing for Rangers. Incidents like the mysterious fire at the stables of Graeme Souness's luxury pad in Edinburgh after Johnston had moved in could have had the striker looking for the next plane out of Scotland. But he stuck it out and, most importantly, played admirably while at Ibrox.

And interestingly, the abuse that players like Neil McCann and Chris Burke have received from the Celtic support for 'turning out for the enemy' in more recent times perhaps shows that the Catholic population is less forgiving than the Protestant one when it comes to players appearing for 'the other side'. Maurice Johnston, though, was the first modern Scottish-born Catholic to put himself in that position, a position that has made it easier for others from the same background to play for Rangers, and for that he deserves great credit.

That said, I wasn't particularly offended by Rangers' anti-Catholic policy in the first place. It was what the club had done for a number of years and, as a boy and a teenager, I was prepared to accept that. But times change. If the club still adopted the policy today, however, I wouldn't hold the same opinion now that I am older and wiser. The society we live in now is far more multi-racial and cosmopolitan than it was when my gran was growing up and the club had to change to reflect that. In football terms, Rangers still represents the Protestant population of Glasgow and beyond, but it does it in a far better way now. Some will never forgive Souness for signing Johnston; personally I can't thank him enough. In fact, I can genuinely say that I got more upset at Dick Advocaat's persistence in making white socks a regular part of the home kit than I did at the arrival of Johnston. Some traditions have to go; but not the black-and-red socks, Dick.

9

A SACRIFICIAL LAMB:
THE DONALD FINDLAY AFFAIR

Colin Glass

I was not present at the Edmiston Club (formerly the Rangers Social Club) on that infamous cup-final party-night on 29 May 1999 when Rangers vice-chairman Donald Findlay would make national news by singing a few songs. But I have attended several others in that venue, so I am well placed to contextualise and comment on the whole sorry affair. It is important, though, to be aware of the full background leading up to this event, as it will facilitate a clearer understanding of exactly what happened, why it happened and all its ramifications

This potion started brewing in the 1970s when the social club opened and although attended on week nights by many who were neither Rangers, nor even football, supporters, most of the custom on match days, naturally, came from fans attending games at Ibrox. I can well recall attending cup-final party-nights which were pretty much like any other Saturday night, with contemporary music from a resident band, followed by a cabaret act. Then, later in the evening, we got what we really wanted when the team would come in with the Scottish Cup.

In a city where Rangers supporters are denied the right to see their team parade trophies through the streets on an open-top bus this type of celebratory event was the nearest many fans would get to really showing their appreciation for the players who had bought them the bragging rights across the country for the next year.

Naturally, the crowd, well lubricated by the time their heroes came in, would go into raptures, and with everyone in musical mode, and a live microphone beckoning, it would only be a matter of minutes before one or two of the players – themselves well-oiled from their own private party in the stadium next door – would be up giving it 'Follow, Follow', 'Who's that team they call the Rangers?' or even, as was the case with the likes of Derek Johnstone, 'The Sash'. However, there were never any paramilitary implications or sinister connotations about the evening and invariably a great night would be had by all.

Scottish society, though, is now plagued by a culture of double standards and resentment of success, especially towards Rangers, and this is exemplified by the modern media.

I can well recall, for example, the build-up to the 1978 Scottish Cup final, when Rangers had pipped Aberdeen for the league title, but had also to play them again in the Hampden showpiece to clinch the treble. Unsurprisingly, many elements in the media were not only rooting for a Rangers defeat (can't have them winning both cups as well as the league) but also were happy to endorse the Dons manager, and former Celtic captain, Billy McNeill's claim that they were, 'going to bring the cup back up north'.

The match itself saw Rangers simply play Aberdeen off the park with some wonderful football; young midfielder Robert Russell was particularly outstanding. The Gers had won the treble again, and yet what did we get in the press the next day? 'Rangers – Kings of Scottish Football' or 'The Blue Masterclass'? Anything praiseworthy at all? No, what we got was headlines such as, 'Aberdeen's big freeze'. The media, unable to admit their error in tipping the Pittodrie men for victory – and unwilling to give

Rangers any credit for a magnificent achievement – tried to take the shine off by offering excuses for the Dons' failure to compete.

An unforgiving and often hostile media have also singled out Ibrox players, officials and fans as 'the bad guys' knowing the impotent public-relations department makes the club a soft touch. Incidents where Rangers players and fans have been unjustifiably savaged in print are too numerous to mention, but three memorable ones that do spring to mind form a foreboding background.

Dutch striker Ronald de Boer was photographed in a Glasgow hotel with a Rangers fan from Belfast who just happened to be Michael Stone, a man who had killed three people at an IRA funeral in the Milltown cemetery in 1988. How was de Boer supposed to know that? Of course he wasn't but it didn't stop the media inferring that Rangers players supported Ulster paramilitaries.

Another foreign player – French goalkeeper Lionell Charbonnier – had his photograph taken at Hamilton races with another fan, who it transpired, had a criminal record. Many dubious characters frequent racecourses but the Frenchman knew nothing about this particular person's past, so what was he supposed to do? If he had refused, no doubt some journalist would then have written about the player being rude and treating the fans with contempt. In some instances this may actually be true, but not in this case, and it is incidents like these that evoke sympathy from me for our wealthy superstars; sometimes they just can't win.

Then there was the case of the photograph that showed Rangers legend, John Greig MBE, holding a beer bottle horizontally to his lips at a North American Rangers Supporters Association convention in Canada. It looked as if he was mimicking playing in a flute band. One Sunday tabloid published the photograph years after the event, inferring sectarianism on the part of Greig, and it is one of the few occasions I can ever remember where Rangers Football Club responded strongly to this sort of thing.

Given these examples of an anti-Rangers agenda – in tandem

with an increasing recognition of the legitimacy of virtually every culture in Scotland other than that of the indigenous Scots, which includes of course the Rangers tradition – is it any surprise that some Gers fans have reverted to a pseudo-siege mentality?

Although Findlay's karaoke effort occurred after the 1999 Scottish Cup final, in many ways the build-up to the incident actually started in early 1997. Let me explain. Rangers were motoring towards nine successive SPL championships (which, incidentally, I believe was superior to Celtic's similar feat of 1967–1974 in the old Scottish first division) thus putting an end to over twenty years of taunting from Hoops fans. However, the Parkhead side were thrown something of a lifeline in an otherwise poor season by being given a home draw against Rangers in the Scottish Cup. It was a lifeline they feverishly grabbed but then, after beating Walter Smith's side, the home side, for the first time ever, completed their celebrations by performing a huddle in the centre circle at the end of the match. The provocative gesture was glossed over by the media but would not be forgotten by the Rangers players or their fans.

The following season, 1997/98, saw Celtic win the title for the first time in ten years, and they also got off to a good start in season 1998/99, which included a 5–1 home victory over Rangers in November. This game was refereed by Willie Young, an official still despised by Gers fans after his performance at Parkhead in the Scottish Cup final only six months earlier. In this final he virtually, and single handedly, secured Hearts their victory over Rangers with an early penalty that never was before denying Ally McCoist a late spot-kick that was a stonewaller. Against Celtic, Young sent off Rangers' young central defender Scott Wilson early on, but flatly refused to red card Alan Stubbs, despite the Celtic defender committing no fewer than six bookable offences after having been cautioned earlier. So much for referees favouring Rangers.

However, as the season progressed, Rangers' rich seam of quality players shone through. They picked up the points and were top of the league as they prepared for the final Old Firm league encounter of the season, at Parkhead on 2 May 1999, another date that would become infamous in the annals of Scottish football. Celtic had to win to have any chance of stopping Rangers regaining their title, whereas an Ibrox victory would arithmetically secure the championship for the Teddy Bears.

The build-up to this match was intense even by the usual standards. Strathclyde Police took the almost unprecedented step of sending officers to both Ibrox and Parkhead to remind the players that their actions on the park could (and probably would) lead to serious violence off the park. Restraint was to be the order of the day. For television purposes, the kick-off was scheduled for the early evening, thereby allowing hours of drinking time. This was to have a significant bearing on the events that occurred throughout an ill-tempered day. In summation, Rangers' stunning 3–0 victory was overshadowed by a whole series of nasty scenes, for which the visitors deserved no blame.

Where do you start when cataloguing the incidents that took place that day at Celtic Park?

Referee Hugh Dallas was struck by missiles, mainly coins, thrown by Celtic fans and this led to the official receiving medical treatment during a temporary suspension of the proceedings. After the match, the referee's home was subjected to a sustained fifteen-minute attack by a Celtic season-ticket holder, although, obviously, not the same supporter who fell off the top tier of one of the Parkhead stands in a rage at his side's impending defeat. Despite falling into fans below him and then being stretchered away, his injuries were mostly to his pride. Not for the first time Dallas failed to discharge his duty properly at Parkhead; he should have sent off the Celtic goalkeeper, Stewart Kerr, for deliberate handball outside the penalty area – a mandatory red-card offence.

Celtic defender Stephan Mahe – the main culprit for the trouble, according to the Strathclyde Police post mortem, written by superintendent Daniel Donnelly of E Division in London Road – and team-mate Vidar Riseth were sent off, along with Rod Wallace of Rangers.

The victorious Ibrox players had to dodge missiles, as well as being spat upon, as they made their way to the tunnel after doing their own victory huddle in front of their own fans at full time. The Rangers players were castigated for this gesture in an attempt to shovel some of the blame across the city, but do you remember 1997?

After the ninety minutes of madness had finished, coins worth £78.40 were apparently collected from the Parkhead pitch, an average of over £13 from each of the 'half dozen or so fans' a Celtic spokesman claimed had been throwing them!

To cap it all, there was serious crowd trouble, both outside the stadium, in the city centre and all over Scotland that night.

And yet, incredibly, despite all that evidence, the game was labelled 'the Old Firm shame game' when, clearly, it was almost exclusively a Celtic shame game.

But what has all this got to do with Donald Findlay singing Orange songs? Well, quite simply, this particular debacle occurred less than four weeks prior to the two teams meeting again in the Scottish Cup final. And as Rangers, according to many sections of the media, were equally culpable with Celtic, the tension leading up to the final escalated even further. My wife, upon witnessing the hooliganism committed by the Celtic fans on the day they lost their league title, pleaded with me not to take our teenage daughter to Hampden for the final. It was only my personal guarantee that I would keep her away from any places where we could encounter opposition fans that swung the day.

And so my daughter and I went to the final, which was deserv-edly won by Rangers 1–0, courtesy of a Rod Wallace goal. But, on exit-ing Hampden, I remember saying to her, 'Well, that's it, we've won the treble. I wonder what tactic the media will use this time to try and take the shine off it?' How prophetic that remark was.

A few hours later, at the Edmiston Club party night, the Bears are in celebratory mood having just beaten their bitterest rivals to secure yet another treble. A party is in full swing inside Ibrox for the players, officials and their wives, but, in keeping with tradition, some of the players, this time accompanied by Findlay, head off shortly after ten o'clock to join 800 fans next door. As if by magic, they all suddenly appear on stage and then the singing begins in earnest; just like half of Hampden Park some five or six hours earlier, the place was bouncing.

As had happened on many occasions in the past, some punters had brought their video cameras in order to capture the atmosphere and to show the footage to friends at a later date. It was innocent, home-movie stuff and acknowledged as such. This was despite the fact that, in the early 1990s, an unscrupulous 'fan' had approached the *Evening Times* and offered to sell a video of a party for £1,500 – the modern equivalent of thirty pieces of silver.

However, the *Evening Times* journalist, much to his credit, stalled the culprit (a different individual to the protagonist in the Findlay affair) in order to 'clear things with his editor' and next day there was a front page story entitled, 'Rangers Rat in Video Sting'. I can readily recall the comments of a Celtic supporter in my work at the time: 'Is that all? A Rangers player singing Orange songs at a Rangers supporters' function? Big deal – our lot do it as well.'

Fast forward to 1999 when, after accepting the microphone from one of the players, Findlay clears his throat. The crowd chants: 'Donald, Donald, give us "The Sash".' Donald duly obliges and the rest, as they say, is history.

There is a recurring debate in the media and elsewhere about song lyrics sung in a football context. Are the Tartan Army both racist and homophobic because they sing, 'We hate Jimmy Hill, he's a poof'? As for singing the 'Billy Boys' with the line, 'up to our knees in Fenian blood' I believe that as a Rangers director, even at a private party, Findlay was injudicious. But it would have been considerably worse if he had sung about 'Catholic blood'.

I am one of many Rangers fans and others who do not equate Fenians with Catholics. Fenians, by definition, are committed to the removal of British jurisdiction from both parts of Ireland by violent means. I have friends who are Catholics but none who are Fenians, just as I have no friends who support the PLO, ETA or any other murder gang. Disliking Fenians, some of whom are Protestants, may have nothing to do with football but it is perfectly natural, just like disliking Nazis. The fact that our greatest rivals espouse Fenianism is the link in this case.

Obviously, this distinction was not shared by the so-called Rangers fan from Erskine, who literally turned up at the *Daily Record's* offices that night. He had come hotfoot along Paisley Road West with a video showing Findlay singing 'The Sash' and other songs, and struck a deal with them for a reputed £6,000. That particular newspaper had been desperately scratching around for an angle to take the shine off Rangers' latest achievements and so when this fellow – who, as they say, 'is known to the police' – walked in to their offices that Saturday night, they could hardly believe their luck.

Copies then quickly found their way to both the BBC and ITV networks but, ironically, even more quickly to Baird's Bar in Glasgow's Gallowgate – a Celtic stronghold – where regulars were able to watch the whole episode before it broke on national television.

The story was splashed across the front page of the *Record* on the Monday, and spread like wildfire across the country. All hell broke loose. The politically correct brigade feigned moral outrage at the contents of the video. Those who had argued that Rangers 'were equally to blame' for the 'Old Firm shame game' – on the basis that the Ibrox players had performed a mock huddle – quickly leapt on to the bandwagon jostling for space alongside those who weren't Celtic supporters but who simply didn't like the Gers, full stop.

The episode was given huge coverage in other newspapers and on national television. And with the media scenting blood, there was no shortage of volunteers ready to move in for the kill. Among them

– although by no means the worst – was Alan Davidson, a sports-writer with Glasgow's *Evening Times* since the seventies. He wrote:

> . . . at last, the Orange Pimpernel has been unveiled and exposed as the bigot he is. Donald Findlay QC was forced into a humiliating resignation yesterday. He jumped before he was pushed by his Rangers chairman, David Murray.
>
> Findlay, with his ludicrous mutton-chop side-burns and fob watch tucked neatly into the waistcoat of his pin-stripe suit was always an accident, or indeed, a disaster waiting to happen for the Ibrox club. His view of life, which involved what he determines to be his love of Rangers, has always been warped. He does not, and never shall, recognise that sport is an entertainment and not some kind of crazy allusion to a world he sees fit only for those who share his beliefs. He was caught out, caught out big time, by an amateur video after Rangers had won the Tennent's Scottish Cup against their ancient rivals at the new Hampden on Saturday. Later Findlay sang hideous sectarian songs at a celebration to mark the club's success. And this from a man who purports to support the law of the land and the freedom of individuals to be given an even break. Findlay has been exposed as a charlatan, a man who claims to provide honour and justice for all, but who, in what he considers to be private moments, is nothing other than the most crass reflection of the illness, the disease that has afflicted our country, and especially Glasgow, for centuries. He is, clearly, an educated man; just as obviously, he lacks the intelligence that can cross the great divide of sectarianism here. Just why he saw fit to sing such ridiculous anthems is unclear. But then again, when you look around the heavy-money seats at Ibrox and at Celtic Park, you witness people of business and social standing who lose the plot.
>
> They may be pillars of the community, but when they

take off the working togs and support their teams the vitriol and the bile re-emerge. They are throwbacks to ancient times and to causes that have no relevance whatsoever in our society. Donald Findlay QC, an advocate and a man who should have been capable of standing aside from such non-sense, has embarrassed himself, the process of law and the nation. Okay, he has done the decent thing by falling on his sword, but his behaviour remains unforgivable.

Davidson, in twisting the knife into Findlay, not only indulged in what some people saw as character assassination but also on a wider scale, and in the eyes of many Rangers fans, reflected the increasing tensions surrounding Protestantism and its place along-side Rangers Football Club in modern-day Scotland.

Some fans believed that Murray had no option than to secure Findlay's resignation, while others believed the vice-chairman was 'hung out to dry'. Yet others viewed it as a form of poetic justice, as Findlay had been very supportive of Murray during some controversial AGMs when Findlay actually conducted the meeting on behalf of his chairman. And yet here he was, effectively sacked by the man he had always backed to the hilt, often in the face of fierce criticism. My own view has not wavered since that day. I believe that in acting as he did, Murray ensured that Donald Findlay was offered up as a sacrificial lamb to those who despise Rangers Football Club, its success and its supporters. The phrase 'If we keep running, they'll keep chasing' springs to mind whenever I reflect on the issue.

For the next five years or so Findlay became a virtual recluse, opting out of the limelight as he wrestled with his demons. But what does the former vice-chairman think about it now? I managed to contact Findlay via a fellow Rangers Supporters Trust board member who had attended and spoken at various functions with him and, probably because of that connection, he reluctantly agreed to be interviewed. (Ironically it was the week after a court ruled that singing 'The Sash' was not a sectarian act.)

I had been no fan of the high-profile QC during his time at Ibrox. I have always had a moral difficulty with the Findlays of this world, but only because I believe it is the duty of the judicial system to keep evil and dangerous people in prison, and the rest of us safe from their behaviour. Findlay and his ilk make money, and a lot of money, from defending some of the most sinister elements in Scottish society, striving to keep them at liberty, while the rest of us would happily see them locked up with the key thrown away. So I was intrigued ahead of our meeting, for more than one reason.

Findlay had just come from another day's work at the High Court in Glasgow when we met in the Marriott hotel. Having successfully rebuilt his life after what were clearly traumatic events for him he seemed to be in no mood to rekindle the dying embers of this particular fire. But once he started talking, I found both him, and his experience, fascinating.

After being made a Rangers director in 1992 during one of the best periods in the club's history he was clearly hurt by the fallout from this episode, losing both his directorship at the club, as well as the position of Lord Rector at St Andrews University. His public humiliation was completed when he was also fined £3,000 by the Faculty of Advocates.

Findlay, like me, had not been brought up in a family of bluenoses. His father took him to see Rangers play at Dens Park as a youngster and he was 'thoroughly bored' with the whole affair.

However, Findlay developed a passion for Rangers. But was this a healthy interest? 'There is a clear difference between being for something as against something' he said, claiming he has had no problems with Celtic fans as a result of that fateful night. Displaying a very laid-back attitude to life, he went on to tell of a Celtic Supporters Club that wrote to him at the time, saying, 'You're an orange bastard, and we know you're an orange bastard, but you're our orange bastard, so don't let the media get you down!'

It had been my suspicion that Findlay felt let down by his

chairman at the time of the incident but at no time during our discussion was he in any way critical of Rangers, or any of its players, officials, directors or fans. 'I believe in loyalty' he said simply. An interesting turn of phrase some might think but, contrary to popular myth, Donald Findlay is not a staunch Protestant. Indeed, he claims to be a lifelong atheist, or at least, 'for as long I remember being able to think for myself. If I was forced to choose just one religion, it would probably be Buddhism.'

On the thorny issues of songs and chants I then asked him how he felt about fans singing 'The Sash' at Ibrox nowadays? 'I have no views on this' he replied, 'No views at all.' Such reticence may indicate that he was being uncooperative but I don't believe that to be the case. He has obviously been soured by the whole affair and, although quite irritated at its regular resurrection in the public domain, his attitude stops some way short of paranoia, although even that could be understandable given the intensity of the media intrusion into all aspects of his life since that infamous night.

I asked him about his views on the signing of Maurice Johnston for Rangers – often a useful barometer for measuring fans' attitudes (and covered in another chapter in this book). He stated that while he was initially against the signing he had changed his mind, due to the player's phenomenal work rate and the clear evidence that he 'played for the jersey'. He also claimed that his opposition to Johnston was not based on religious grounds, but because of the player's previous connections and conduct with Celtic.

I have to say I unreservedly believe him. It has become tiresome for Rangers fans constantly to be accused of bigotry simply for disliking their rivals. Inter Milan fans do not like AC Milan, Sheffield United fans do not like Sheffield Wednesday; such is the nature of football rivalry. Celtic FC, and their supporters, have got to grow up and learn to accept warranted criticism, without always screaming 'prejudice' or playing the bigotry card.

But what else does Donald Findlay hold dear? A passionate

believer in the concept of individual liberty, he believes that everyone should have the right to walk anywhere, within the law. He described to me how, after the collapse of the Berlin Wall, he walked through the Brandenburg gate, and how that was an emotional experience for him. He was learning to fly (coincidentally at the same flying club where I am a member) but abandoned that project when the storm broke.

Several months after Findlay's resignation the Rangers chairman, David Murray, told a packed Royal Concert Hall in Glasgow, during the club's one hundredth annual meeting:

> Let's not forget that Donald Findlay is a personal friend of mine and it was me who invited him to join the board. When the story broke Donald was distraught. We had a meeting and he decided to do the honourable thing and resign. It is an unfortunate side to certain sections of the media today that they like to give some people a doing. But if you are vice-chairman of Rangers and in the public eye you have a responsibility and shouldn't do such things. However, as far as I am concerned he has done his penance and as a season-ticket holder he is welcome back to Ibrox to sit in his seat.

The key phase appears to be 'as a season-ticket holder' and, unsurprisingly, this not an option which Donald Findlay exercises to any great extent these days. He hardly ever goes to Ibrox now, although he did return to the first home game after the incident in July 1999, which was Ian Ferguson's testimonial 'because I said I would'. Nowadays, his Rangers 'duties' mainly focus on attending Rangers Football Club roadshows with former international winger, Willie Henderson, and appearing, almost Bernard Manning-style, at Rangers Supporters Club functions.

Donald Findlay is no bigot; that shone through loud and clear in my interview with him. His birthday is on 17 March (St Patrick's day) while one of his friends from the legal profession – a Celtic fan

– has his birthday on 12 July; so they agreed to swap! No harm there, everyone has a laugh and yet there are those (on the 'offended bus') who condemn such light-heartedness? He struck me as a man who is now at peace with himself. He knows he is no bigot, and knows that those close to him know that too. As far as those who have labelled him as such, well, the impression I got was that, without being arrogant, he genuinely doesn't care.

But lest the reader disregards my thoughts on the Findlay affair as those of a fawning Rangers fan desperate to cover up an embarrassing incident, I conducted a straw poll of other bluenoses. It was admittedly an unscientific exercise but, nevertheless, I believe there are many who consider Murray to have misjudged the situation when he allowed Findlay to go.

I contend that the comments of the two fans below, Steve Tyrie and Gordon Semple, are broadly representative of the opinions of the mainstream Rangers support on this issue.

What did they think of Findlay's behaviour that night at the Edmiston Club and was it a resigning matter? Stevie Tyrie:

> I didn't think anything of it because I was doing exactly the same, as were Rangers supporters all over the world. Findlay was, and is, a Rangers supporter and was celebrating a win over Celtic that gave Rangers the treble. He was perfectly entitled to celebrate and I certainly didn't think the songs he was singing were in any way out of place in a Rangers Supporters Club. It wasn't as if he was running up into a Celtic area of the city doing that. He was surrounded by Rangers supporters in a Rangers environment and doing nothing wrong so I don't think he did anything to merit resigning.

Gordon Semple added:

> There is an argument that his behaviour was unbecoming for a Rangers director, and whilst I can understand this point

of view, the troops often like to see one of those from atop the marble staircase within Ibrox identify with the punters and Donald Findlay was doing just that – with gusto. He felt pressure to resign from Murray and so he did the honourable thing, and fell on his sword. The alternative was to sit tight, let the storm pass and live to fight another day. In the longer run this would have damaged the club less, but the desire to pander to the Scottish media was irresistible and so Findlay was sacrificed to save the club's reputation. With hindsight, it's almost certain that the enforced resignation of Findlay has harmed the club far more than if he'd remained on the Rangers board. It's worth noting that one of Donald Findlay's biggest allies at this difficult time was none other than Michael Kelly, the former Celtic director. One can't help feeling that there was a 'there but for the grace of God go I' motivation for this. I'd be surprised if, over the years, Celtic directors haven't enjoyed the occasional sing-song which they would have preferred hadn't been broadcast on national television. But as far as I'm concerned, Celtic directors can indulge themselves all they want at functions for those who support that club.

But weren't his actions proof that Rangers FC is a sectarian organisation? Semple's reply was an unequivocal 'No', while Tyrie argued:

It depends what context the word 'sectarian' is being used in. If it's pertaining to its meaning 'sect' then yes, as it emphasizes the links Rangers undeniably have with the Protestant/ Orange community. If it's being used in its pejorative context then the answer is emphatically no. If anybody has problems with songs about historical battles and incidents then I'd suggest they're the ones who are being sectarian in the way they'd accuse Findlay of being.

Once again when faced with a contentious issue, the question boils down to how Rangers handled the whole affair. And what the repercussions were in terms of the club's reputation. Semple again:

I was extremely disappointed. All too often our club caves in when a battle has to be fought. The Duncan Ferguson situation, where the player ended up going to jail, is just one example, and the Scottish football authorities' extremely harsh treatment of Graeme Souness, is another. Ironically, Donald Findlay, one of Scotland's finest legal minds, could and should have defended Duncan Ferguson in a case which would have been won in a canter, but the club chose to do nothing, and the player was made a scapegoat. But the karaoke incident certainly didn't enhance the club's reputation in the wider world, and it gave partisan media an opportunity to twist the knife and put the boot into a club many of them openly despise. Sadly, David Murray has never quite understood the nature of the hostility towards the club he owns, and he's been loathe to tackle the perpetrators. Rangers, like Manchester United, attract sizeable media interest and those who don't love the club usually detest the club's very existence. For many in Scotland, when it comes to Rangers, there's no neutral position.

Tyrie was similarly enraged:

The way the club handled it was a disgrace. They surrendered to enemies of Rangers and that is unforgivable. The thing is, Findlay was hung out to dry by Rangers because they thought he should resign but a journalist who, two years later, laughed at the Ibrox Disaster, had no action taken against him at all. I found that sickening. What's the worse crime? It was weakness and hypocrisy I never thought I'd see coming from Ibrox. By accepting his resignation, Rangers did untold damage to themselves. By acting this way they were leaving themselves wide open to whatever the media wanted to say about them. If they'd stood up for him they wouldn't have lost the confidence of a big number of Rangers fans and they'd have shown themselves to have character to a wider audience. As it was they backed themselves into a corner by admitting Rangers were everything the media accused them of being.

For the most part, I concur with Semple and Tyrie. In the case of Donald Findlay, QC and former vice-chairman of Rangers, we have Scottish double standards at their worst.

Previously lauded by the media, his ability to keep a murderer out of jail made Findlay some sort of hero – but heaven forbid that he sing a few songs among fellow Rangers fans the night we win a treble.

As a Rangers director, never mind vice-chairman, he should have been aware that he would have been constantly under the spotlight and could never afford to be caught off guard; it goes with the territory. Was he naïve? Yes. Was it injudicious? Probably. Was it a hanging offence? Certainly not.

Was it a day that shook Rangers? Yes it was, but only because of the way the club allowed it to be handled. Everyone makes mistakes in their life, and Donald Findlay could have been allowed to apologise for any offence caused – although nobody who was there complained – and still retain his position.

The witch-hunt against Findlay apparently continues unabated. In May 2005, six years after his resignation, he was again being hung out to dry by the Scottish media and his colleagues at the Faculty of Advocates following a joke he made about the Pope at a Rangers Supporters Club function in Northern Ireland. While some might say he is a fool unto himself for this, the only individual who took offence was the undercover journalist who attended the event. Apparently his fellow advocates think it is laudable for him to try to help Celtic fan and child murderer Luke Mitchell escape justice in the High Court. But to include the Pope in his stand-up comedy routine – which also pokes fun at the police, women and masons, among others – is worthy of reprimand. Curious lot, our advocates. But then, we now live in a curious country.

10

BACK FROM THE BRINK

Lisa Gray

On 11 December 2001, when it was announced that Rangers manager Dick Advocaat would be standing down as Ibrox boss, the Dutchman's abdication came with more of a whimper rather than the bang you would expect from the man dubbed the Little General.

The story, it could be argued, hardly merits being described as a day that shocked Rangers in the way the title of this book suggests. Certainly, it failed to grab the headlines in the same way that Mo Johnston's signing had in the summer of 1989. Moreover, the immediate on-field implications of Advocaat's retreat were far less severe than that moment in December 1964 when Jim Baxter broke his leg in Austria against Rapid Vienna, leaving historians and fans pondering for years to come if Rangers could have been the first British team to lift the European Cup instead of Celtic. And there was obviously none of the depression that followed the Ibrox disaster in 1971 when sixty-six fans lost their lives in a stairway crush following the Old Firm's New Year derby.

But the truth is that Advocaat's three-and-a-half-year reign rocked the club to its very foundations and the legacy of that controversial period in Rangers history is still reverberating around the bowels of Ibrox to this day. The appointment of the Dutchman's chosen successor, Alex McLeish, signalled an end to the free-spending days that almost ruined the club. A new, more frugal era had begun in Govan.

There were, of course, incredible highs during the former PSV Eindhoven coach's time in Glasgow. Winning the treble in his first season in charge is an accomplishment no-one can ever take away from Advocaat and it was no mean feat either when you consider the rebuilding process he took on following the famous nine-in-a-row era of Walter Smith. Gone were Ibrox heroes such as Ally McCoist, Richard Gough and Andy Goram, and in their place was a far more 'continental' side with players who knew they had to bring success to Rangers if they were to have any hope of being accepted by the Ibrox faithful. Almost a whole new team arrived at Ibrox and men like Giovanni van Bronckhorst, Arthur Numan, Claudio Reyna and Stefan Klos quickly realised only one outcome in Scotland is acceptable – being number one.

The new-look Gers side dutifully delivered the League Cup, the Scottish Cup and the biggest prize of all in the shape of the league championship. And, despite having lost the 'tenth' title to their Parkhead rivals the previous season, there was little doubt that the pendulum of power had just swung right back to Rangers. However, while this latest round of success was costing the Ibrox club more than ever before ambition, big-name players and the sense that a new era was about to get underway under Advocaat was nothing the Rangers fans hadn't already seen before under different leadership.

Souness had been there, done it and worn the football shirt for Liverpool, Sampdoria and Scotland when he arrived like a whirl-wind at Ibrox in 1986. It was a time when society in general was obsessed with money. The Tories were in power, with Margaret Thatcher at the helm, yuppies roamed the streets of London with briefcases and new-fangled devices called mobile phones and the ultimate story of greed and power, *Wall Street*, was set to take cinemas by storm. It's hardly surprising that so many people were willing to buy into the 'big club' mentality that Souness was so keen to instil at Rangers and that meant big money to back up his plans.

The Ibrox player-manager pulled off the unthinkable – convincing top stars such as Terry Butcher, Chris Woods and Ray Wilkins to leave England behind in favour of Scottish football. The revolution gathered even more pace when arch-capitalist David Murray took control of the club in 1988 and Souness was given even bigger budgets to cement the club's domestic supremacy for the next decade or so.

Fast-forward to the summer of 1998 and the similarities between the Souness reign and Advocaat's stormy tenure are plain to see. The only major difference was that the former coach of the Dutch national team was casting his net further afield than England, with the perhaps inevitable result that the debt would eventually assume monstrous proportions. Footballers' wages were spiralling out of control all over Europe but, at Ibrox, this was being ignored in pursuit of the ultimate goal: European success. And, for a while, everyone at Ibrox was willing to go along for the ride.

Initially, everything went to plan. The first-season treble was followed by more signings and a league and Scottish Cup double in 1999/2000. In contrast to the euphoria in Govan at that time, Celtic had become something of a laughing stock after appointing Liverpool legend John Barnes as manager alongside former Hoops hero Kenny Dalglish in the newly created role of director of football operations.

The reason behind putting together this unlikely 'dream team' was as an antidote to the uninspiring administration of Dr Jozef Venglos. The good doctor may have possessed a philosophy that would have sent most people into a state of unconsciousness but the Barnes-Dalglish partnership soon turned into a nightmare. By the time the struggling Hoops were slaughtered by first division outfit Inverness Caledonian Thistle in the third round of the Scottish Cup at Celtic Park on 8 February 2000 – which inspired the unforgettable newspaper headline 'Super Caley go Ballistic, Celtic are Atrocious' – the writing was on the wall for Barnes.

The former England international was soon back down the M74 to England, followed by King Kenny at the end of the season, to bring to an end an amusing episode that only strengthened Rangers' claim to be the top team in Scotland. But, all the while, expectations in Govan were getting higher and Advocaat was spending more and more to achieve his lofty ambitions. In hindsight, season 1999/2000 was the pinnacle of Advocaat's reign. After disposing of FC Haka and UEFA Cup holders Parma in the Champions League qualifiers, Rangers narrowly failed to progress from a group that included Valencia, Bayern Munich and PSV Eindhoven, even though the Dutch side were beaten home and away. The Ibrox club then dropped down to the UEFA Cup where they were unlucky to be beaten on penalties by Borussia Dortmund.

Rangers looked set to go from strength to strength but something happened in the summer of 2000 that would change everything in the Old Firm world – Irishman Martin O'Neill was appointed boss at Celtic. It was, arguably, an appointment that signalled the beginning of the end for Advocaat. While the Rangers manager was focusing on the European dream, O'Neill quickly set about dismantling the Ibrox side's domestic domination.

Jim Templeton, president of the Rangers Supporters Assembly, admits the arrival of O'Neill exposed Advocaat's grasp on Scottish football as little more than a house of cards, that folded with the first strong breeze:

> I believe he thought the Scottish fringe players would be good enough to win Rangers the league and the big foreign names would be kept for the big games when they were needed. Then we hit this horrendous run of injuries and, very quickly, it was proved that the Scottish players who were brought in weren't up to the job. To be truthful, I think

he lost the plot. Prior to Martin O'Neill coming, there was no competition – they would run us close for a few months and gradually they would fall away. When Martin O'Neill came in, all of a sudden they looked like they were going to be a real threat. Advocaat became his own worst enemy.

Advocaat had proved himself to be a big player in the transfer market, initially spending £36.5 million on rebuilding the squad he inherited from Walter Smith. He then bolstered it over the next couple of summers, apparently free from any financial restrictions. However, even he shattered everyone's expectations in the run-up to Christmas 2000. David Murray had once famously proclaimed that for every fiver Celtic spent, Rangers would spend a tenner. But no-one believed he would keep his word as unequivocally as he did that November, when Rangers made Scottish football history.

Celtic had broken the Scottish transfer record in the summer of 2000, when O'Neill convinced the Parkhead purse-bearers to part with £6 million to secure the services of former Blackburn and Chelsea striker Chris Sutton, a player who would prove to be more than value for money. Not content with merely matching such heady levels of spending, however, Advocaat completely obliterated the Celtic record when Murray sanctioned the £12.5 million purchase of Chelsea hitman, Tore Andre Flo. The Norwegian made his debut against Celtic at Ibrox and, in truly dramatic style, grabbed a goal as Rangers romped to an emphatic 5–1 victory that helped to erase the memory of the 6–2 spanking at Parkhead earlier in the season.

But it wasn't long before the realisation set in down the Copland Road that – despite being a decent enough player with a respectable goal-scoring return – Flo would never live up to his hefty price tag. Indeed, fears were beginning to grow that he would prove to be nothing more than a very costly mistake.

Former Rangers player and now football agent, Gordon Smith, believes the decision to recruit Flo also led to dangerous assumptions about the financial health of Rangers at that time. This was despite evidence that they were hurtling towards a record debt, a debt that would reach a staggering £73.9 million by June 2004:

> It was a watershed moment. People thought they could afford it but it subsequently proved that Rangers were spending money they didn't have and the debts were spiralling as a result. He was a very good player and it wasn't his fault that he had this 'waste of money' tag – it's very hard to fulfil that potential and justify having that amount of money spent on you. But as soon as Celtic won the treble, the writing was on the wall. Tore Andre Flo was seen as a panic buy.

However, even as Advocaat's empire appeared to be crumbling around him, the Little General defiantly pushed on with his European dream. More players were brought in during the summer of 2001 and, although Celtic forged ahead at the start of the season, who could forget that winter night on 6 December 2001 when Rangers finally breached the third round of the UEFA Cup following the most dramatic of penalty shoot-out victories over Paris St Germain at the Parc des Princes? But then who would have predicted Advocaat would no longer be at the helm for the fourth-round tie against Feyenoord?

The Dutchman announced he was quitting to 'move upstairs' to join the Rangers hierarchy in the newly-created role of director of football. He would also commit himself to the part-time role of Holland coach following the resignation of Louis van Gaal, a job that would eventually provide the justification for leaving Rangers permanently.

Advocaat has already bitterly denied his decision to quit the Ibrox dugout was a direct result of the O'Neill revolution across the city. In a book about that period, *The Advocaat Years*, he stated:

Listen, I have a big reputation and you don't become the manager of Holland twice just because you are a nice man. I'm a well-known manager in Europe, everyone knows me – not everyone can say that. I have nothing against Martin O'Neill and I have to be fair and say that he brought in some good players – like Thompson, Lennon, Hartson, Sutton – and they were never injured. Those players always played so in that way you can say he did better than me in transfers. . . . Because of the luck Celtic had, Larsson played for seven years and in that time he was almost never injured. There's no doubt that was the difference between the teams because, at the other end we had a better side, but Larsson made the difference. O'Neill showed he is a good manager but I have shown that I am a good manager as well.

Rangers season-ticket holder Scott Gray disagrees with the Dutchman's claim that O'Neill played no part in his decision to cut and run:

I think Advocaat's decision to step down as manager was no bad thing. Whilst he undoubtedly brought the club much success during his reign, the best years appeared to be behind him. I wonder if he had the heart for the new challenge which had presented itself in the shape of Martin O'Neill. Perhaps this, coupled with the tightening of the purse strings at Ibrox, was a bridge too far.

Gray's assertion regarding the changing financial situation in football is pertinent. The latter part of season 2001/02 had proved to be one of the most tumultuous ever experienced by Scottish football's top flight as the issue of television money began dominating the back pages. The SPL had enjoyed the handouts from a Sky Sports deal worth a record-breaking £45 million in June 1998 but, with that deal set to expire, it emerged that all twelve club chairmen had unanimously agreed to forge ahead with plans for their own dedicated television channel. The channel was the brainchild of then SPL chief executive, Roger Mitchell, and was supposed to be the financial saviour for all the clubs – not just Glasgow's big two. But it wasn't long before the cracks began to appear in that assumption.

In March 2002, Bradford chairman Geoffrey Richmond had warned the SPL to learn lessons from England following the demise of ITV Digital, a development that had a catastrophic effect on lower-league clubs down south. Within days, the Old Firm wrote to the ten other clubs to voice concerns over the deal before pulling the plug completely on 8 April. BBC Scotland entered into a bidding war for the television rights and, when Sky made it clear they were not interested, a two-year-deal with the BBC was signed at the end of July just before the season began in earnest. The BBC contract was much less lucrative than the previous Sky deal and it was becoming clear that a bleak financial future lay ahead for the SPL clubs. The gravy train was about to hit the buffers. And Rangers would suffer more than most.

The pivotal day – Advocaat's departure – had already passed some months earlier. Significantly, the Dutchman's successor would not to be drawn from Europe's elite. Those days were over. Alex McLeish, then the Hibs manager, was regarded as nothing short of underwhelming in most quarters. Did he really have the credentials to become the eleventh manager of one of the most famous clubs in Europe?

Advocaat and Murray certainly thought so, but the fans were far from convinced. Templeton admits the appointment of McLeish split the Rangers support down the middle with 'probably 50 per cent believing he was not up to the job'. Lifelong Rangers supporter Elaine Sommerville is less constrained: 'I wanted a bigger name to take over so I was not too impressed and I think my friends felt the same.'

While the Ibrox faithful were warily eyeing their new manager,

Advocaat had quietly retreated to the safety of his new office within the wood-panelled corridors of Ibrox stadium. Which begs the question: why exactly was the role of director of football created for Dick Advocaat? To smooth his exit from Rangers is the simple answer, according to Jim Templeton: 'The club had survived for over 100 years without a director of football. I don't think it was the Rangers way to just show people the door and that job was almost like a halfway house.'

Dougie Stanforth believes retaining the services of Advocaat served the dual purpose of acting as a security blanket for those fans unconvinced by McLeish's ability successfully to assume the manager's role, while paving the way for the Dutchman's low-key departure: 'When I heard McLeish was to be appointed as manager I thought this was too big a risk for a team like Rangers and was happy that we had some security in the fact that Advocaat was staying on and could still have a hand in the team.'

Advocaat's last game was, ironically, against now managerless Hibs on 12 December 2001, the day following the announcement he was being replaced by McLeish. It was a low-key changeover to say the least. The new Gers boss was introduced to the crowd who seemed none too enthused and when the final whistle went after a 1–1 draw, the Little General retreated up the tunnel almost unnoticed.

McLeish had had the look of a rabbit caught in the headlights when he was unveiled as Rangers manager as though he, like everyone else, could barely believe what was happening. A stuttering 2–2 draw against another former club, Motherwell, at Fir Park in his first game in charge hardly augured well for the future.

With what was still Advocaat's squad, McLeish set about proving that he did not need Uncle Dick looking over his shoulder as he put his own stamp on the club. Any realistic hope of catching Celtic in the title race had evaporated but two cup triumphs that season soon had the fans on his side.

A CIS Insurance Cup semi-final win over Celtic at Hampden in

February 2002, courtesy of an astonishing winner from the hapless Bert Konterman, provided McLeish with his first Old Firm victory. The March final provided first division outfit Ayr United with their best day out in living memory but the good men of the Scottish Football League were no doubt ironing the red, white and blue ribbons before the Ibrox side's 4–0 win. Hampden Park was proving to be a happy hunting ground for McLeish and more good times were just around the corner. On 4 May 2002, Peter Lovenkrands's double against Celtic allowed Rangers to secure a last-gasp 3–2 win over their biggest foes in an exciting Scottish Cup final.

As the Danish winger enjoyed the plaudits on that spring day in Glasgow, thunderclouds were gathering over Parkhead as O'Neill contemplated the possibility that he had met his match in Alex McLeish. Jim Divers, secretary of the Celtic Supporters Association, revealed his thoughts on Advocaat's successor:

> I don't think Celtic saw Alex McLeish as a major threat when he took over. Advocaat certainly had a better pedigree than McLeish and the Celtic supporters recognised that McLeish would not be getting the money Advocaat had to spend. He subsequently proved that he could manage with limited money and use Bosmans to his advantage but, although he had done well at provincial clubs, he hadn't enjoyed phenomenal success before joining Rangers. There is always pressure on any manager and even more so when you are the manager of an Old Firm club and that included Dick Advocaat. He found it difficult when Martin O'Neill became the new kid on the block but you would have to say that McLeish proved to be a worthy successor.

But times had changed dramatically at Ibrox as McLeish was finding to his cost. In Advocaat's first season he had secured the services of players such as Arthur Numan, Andrei Kanchelskis and Giovanni van Bronckhorst. Subsequent signings such as Colin Hendry, Allan Johnston, Kenny Miller and Paul Ritchie appeared to be tossed aside in the same way Imelda Marcos might discard a pair of shoes to the back of the wardrobe. Ritchie, quite remarkably, was bought and then sold by Advocaat within a couple of weeks. The turnover of players was frantic and expensive. Further signings such as Fernando Ricksen, Bert Konterman and Michael Ball arrived, all brought for big fees and all enjoying the highest salaries – and not always producing on the park.

In sharp contrast, McLeish headed into his first full campaign as Rangers manager with just two new signings: Mikel Arteta arrived in a £6 million move from Barcelona and Kevin Muscat on a free transfer from Wolves. The capture of Muscat, who flopped spectacu-larly, would be the beginning of a trend that would see McLeish recruit mostly free-transfer men.

Probably the best example of the comparative gulf in cash avail-able to the two managers is in the case of the de Boer brothers. Ronald signed for Rangers two years into Advocaat's reign and commanded impressive wages of £35,000 per week. When McLeish recruited the services of his twin brother, Frank, in January of 2004 his weekly wage was £4,000, which the Rangers boss claimed was 'pocket money'. Although the Ibrox boss would later claim that remark had been tongue-in-cheek, it's clear who would have bought the best presents for mama and papa de Boer the following Christmas.

Nevertheless, Rangers fans were looking for success, not excuses, as they looked ahead to McLeish's first full campaign in charge – and they were not to be disappointed.

The final day of season 2002/03 proved to be so dramatic that even the combined minds of Steven Spielberg, Martin Scorsese and James Cameron would have deemed the events on 25 May too far-fetched for the big screen.

Managers often speak of title races going 'right to the wire' but there is little doubt that Alex McLeish and Martin O'Neill never dreamed for a second that the championship would be decided by a single goal. On the last day, with both Old Firm sides going for goals, Celtic's task was to dismantle Kilmarnock at Rugby Park, while Dunfermline were the visitors at Ibrox.

Michael Mols set the tone with the opener after just three minutes but the relief turned to despair with eleven minutes on the clock when Jason Dair pulled a goal back for Dunfermline. News of a Chris Sutton goal in Ayrshire filtered through a packed Ibrox as nerves began to audibly jangle. And the ninety minutes continued in the same vein as Rangers found the back of the net only to hear the news that Celtic had netted again in Kilmarnock. With the clock running down it was neck and neck. Then referee Stuart Dougal made a decision that greater men than him would have shied away from when he pointed to the penalty spot. As the giant screen at Ibrox showed that ninety minutes had come and gone, Mikel Arteta kept his cool to convert from twelve yards while the whole of Ibrox erupted around him. Celtic had won 4–0 – and missed a penalty – but Rangers' 6–1 victory was enough to take the title. The Ibrox fans were ecstatic and all doubts about McLeish were gone; momentarily.

A 1–0 victory over Dundee in the Scottish Cup final ensured a domestic clean-sweep for McLeish but the Ibrox boss was not naive enough to think that it was going to be plain sailing from then on. He was well aware that he was seen by many as the cheap option, and that the blank cheques made available to Advocaat, Walter Smith and Graeme Souness before him, were no longer a possibility.

The truth about the state of Rangers' finances was finally starting to hit home in the summer of 2003, with debts at Ibrox reported to be creeping up to the £60 million mark. McLeish was forced to wheel and deal in an ever-diminishing transfer market with what was little more than a shoestring budget. Bargain-basement signings with big reputations, such as Emerson and Nuno Capucho, were recruited. And they were complemented by uninspiring journeymen like

Egil Ostenstaad, Zurab Khizanishvili, Paulo Vanoli and Henning Berg, only the latter proving to be anywhere near adequate.

Rangers proved to be a shambles the following season (2003/04) and lost all their trophies, with Celtic taking the title back. Once again questions were being asked of McLeish. Sure, the fans were getting the message about the club's financial plight but what was on show simply wasn't good enough.

Advocaat was by now long gone but the fallout from his reign – particularly the £12 million spent on Flo – still grated with fans who believed the Dutchman had a large part to play in the financial disarray at the club. Gordon Smith, however, believes the Dutchman cannot be held completely accountable for all his purchases. Speculation continues to this day that several players from the Advocaat era were in fact 'Murray signings'. It was Smith who oversaw Kenny Miller's £2 million transfer from Hibs to Rangers in June 2000 and, although unable to say for sure that the Little General never craved the services of the young striker, he confirms that he did not speak with the Dutchman once while the deal was being thrashed out:

It was a strange one. I did all the talking with David Murray and never spoke to Dick Advocaat at any time. I was told he wanted the player and took it as read that the deal was taking place on Advocaat's advice. I couldn't say 100 per cent that he wasn't an Advocaat signing. Maybe he just went off him as a player but at no stage did I speak to Dick Advocaat. Kenny wanted to play for Rangers, he saw it as the big move he was looking for and he was keen to do well there. But he was never given the opportunity to do the job he wanted to do.

Smith believes Murray had no option but to tighten the purse-strings when the Advocaat chapter in Rangers' history came to an end. He added:

There is no question there was a major turnaround and it wasn't a gradual move. After spending £12 million, there was a 'need to cut back' mentality. That meant Alex McLeish had to survive as a coach, while bringing players through at Rangers and searching the Bosman market – a job he has done very well. Things were changing dramatically anyway and the change in manager at Rangers was indicative of the way the game was going. Dick Advocaat was a spending manager – big budgets and large funds – while Alex McLeish's remit was to come in, turns things around and get rid of some of the big-money players without having too much money to spend. It was a total change and Alex McLeish had a very different role to play. The big-spending days of Dick Advocaat were over and, in a way it was a good thing, because it was a situation which had to be addressed.

The times certainly were changing but, in the close season of 2004/ 2005, McLeish was allowed to sign seven players to strengthen his squad in the shape of Nacho Novo, Dado Prso, Jean-Alain Boumsong, Dragan Mladenovic, Marvin Andrews, Alex Rae and Gregory Vignal (on loan from Liverpool). That Boumsong, signed on a Bosman from French side Auxerre, quickly proved to be McLeish's most impressive capture said it all. However, although the budgets may have been lower, the expectations placed on the shoulders of a Rangers manager remain impossibly high.

A goalless draw on the opening day of the season to what would prove to be a rejuvenated Aberdeen side set alarm bells ringing. The subsequent defeat to Celtic to leave Rangers trailing even further in the title race saw alarm turn to panic and, by the time CSKA Moscow sent McLeish's disjointed-looking side out of the Champions League at the qualifying stages, many were already calling for the manager's head on a plate. Enough was enough.

While Celtic were enthusing about being drawn alongside

Barcelona, AC Milan and Shakhtar Donetsk in the group stages of the Champions League, Rangers were making hard work of booking a consolation place in the UEFA Cup. Goals were proving hard to come by for McLeish's new-look front-line and their qualifying double-header against Portuguese side Maritimo was decided by a nerve-wracking penalty shoot-out. It was a game that could have cost McLeish his job – instead Rangers spluttered along for most of the season, seemingly towards another championship failure.

Off the field, attention was focusing more and more on the club's financial problems. The Rangers Supporters Trust had been set up in order to claim a seat on the board but also to face down persistent rumours that the club were set to sell Ibrox to alleviate their debt burden. To allay the fans' fears, David Murray – who had also borne the brunt of some stinging criticisms from the media and supporters regarding his stewardship of the club – made some staggering announcements. He had relinquished the chairmanship to John McClelland in 2002 to concentrate on his other business interests but revealed in September 2004 that he would take over the day to day running of the club again and return to the role of executive chairman.

Murray's company, MHL Limited, had bought ENIC's 20 per cent stake in Rangers for £8.7 million, bringing his own stake in the club to 86 per cent. He also announced plans for a rights issue, which would go on to realise over £51 million. Of this sum, £50 million was underwritten by Murray International Holdings. Murray also spoke of his hope that the club's crippling debt would soon be eradicated.

And, in what seemed like an act of contrition, the Edinburgh businessman held his hand up to mistakes caused by what he called 'over-ambition' when he addressed the club's shareholders at the annual general meeting, while also warning that the big-money transfers were firmly in the past:

We have at times been accused of over-ambition and we were unfortunate that the majority of the long-term debt was incurred by investment in the playing squad when transfer values and player wages were grossly over inflated by the promise of media revenues which failed to materialise. This announcement heralds the beginning of a new chapter in Rangers' history. The financial future will be secured by the rights issue. I have consistently stressed that we will no longer be net spenders in the transfer market and the rights issue is not intended to generate surplus cash at this stage for investment in the playing squad.

Instead, the extra cash for McLeish to spend came at a cost when star defender Boumsong quit Ibrox after just six months at the club for the Barclays Premiership and Newcastle United. Rangers received a healthy £8 million to soften the blow and the cash played a part in the arrival of Thomas Buffel and Sotirios Kyrgiakos and, most notably, the return of prodigal son Barry Ferguson during the January 2005 transfer window.

When Boumsong left Rangers, Celtic were at the top of the table by a single point and now, with their best player gone, there was a fear among fans that the title was starting to slip away. Alarm bells started to ring when Inverness Caledonian Thistle claimed a last-gasp draw at Ibrox and, by the time bottom side Dundee United held on for a 1–0 win at the same venue, many supporters were looking for McLeish's head. A 2–1 defeat in the final Old Firm game of the season seemed to have handed Martin O'Neill's side another championship. At the same time as the league title looked to be heading to Parkhead for the fourth time in five seasons, PSV – who had been hammered 4–1 at Ibrox just five and half years earlier – had regrouped to the extent that they were taking on AC Milan in the Champions League semi-finals. The fortunes of two of Advocaat's former clubs could hardly have differed more.

However, there was to be an incredible end to the season, which put the club's financial woes to the back of fans' minds. And it was so, so unexpected. On the final day, Celtic headed for injury-ravaged Motherwell knowing a win would be enough to see them crowned Scottish champions. At Easter Road, Rangers needed a victory at Hibernian while praying for a miracle at Fir Park. A helicopter was stationed at a secret location, ready to deliver the SPL trophy to the victors, but even the most loyal Rangers fan did not expect the silverware to be making the trip to Leith. A sense of quiet resignation settled over the away fans at Easter Road when news of Chris Sutton's opener at Fir Park filtered through. It was perhaps fitting that Nacho Novo, who had suffered a crisis in front of goal for the previous seven games, found the back of the net for Rangers and Hibs made it clear they were willing to settle for a 1–0 defeat, which would allow them to secure a place in the UEFA Cup at the expense of Aberdeen. For Rangers, though, a win looked likely to be nothing more than a consolation at the end of a season filled with what-ifs. But if the final day of season 2002/03 had been the stuff of fairytales, the events of 22 May 2005 were about to eclipse even that amazing day.

With the game almost at walking pace, an eerie calm had descended over Easter Road but that was suddenly shattered by 5,000 Rangers supporters simultaneously erupting, shocking the players on the park and confusing the home fans. It could mean only one thing: Motherwell had scored and the SPL trophy now had Rangers' name on it. In the end, Terry Butcher's men did not just settle for the draw; they went the whole hog by romping to victory. Striker Scott McDonald – an Australian with a Celtic-supporting father and a bluenose mother – grabbed two goals in the final two minutes to ensure his life would never be the same again. Incredibly, Rangers were champions.

There was another blow in store for Celtic when O'Neill confirmed he would be quitting as manager after the Hoops' Scottish

Cup final win against Dundee United. Reports emerged that the Northern Irishman would take a break from the game to care for his sick wife, Geraldine, and the worst fears of the Parkhead faithful were confirmed at a press conference a few days before the Hampden showpiece. Hoops chiefs attempted to soften the blow by naming Gordon Strachan as O'Neill's successor. A red-headed star of the Aberdeen European Cup Winners' Cup side of 1983, who had gone on to enjoy a reasonably successful, if rather unspectacular, managerial career until being given the opportunity to manage one of the top clubs in Scotland. Sound familiar?

Peter Rafferty, secretary of the Affiliation of Celtic Supporters Associations, claims Strachan will be given the backing of the fans – but only if he can deliver the domestic and European success they crave. Hardly a ringing endorsement. He said: 'We believe he is the right man to replace Martin O'Neill. But, even though the fans are patient people, they will expect him to win the championship this season.'

Others were less diplomatic. Jim Burns phoned the *Daily Record* to say that he 'hadn't met a Celtic fan who thinks Strachan is up to the job' while Colin McKenzie complained: 'The appointment of Strachan is a throwback to the old biscuit-tin days. We should have spent money and brought in Davie Moyes (Everton), one of the best managers in Britain.'

In stark contrast to the fanfare that greeted O'Neill's arrival, Strachan had to settle for around fifty curious fans awaiting his first visit to Parkhead as Celtic manager. He may soon discover that a similar background is not all he shares with former teammate and good friend McLeish – he may also find that the road to winning acceptance is a long and hazardous one.

McLeish described the moment Motherwell equalised against Celtic on the final day as the 'biggest spine-tingler of my life' but did Rangers fans reflect on the achievement and finally concede that the former Hibs and Motherwell boss had been the right man for the job all along? John Macmillan, secretary of the Rangers Supporters Association, is optimistic:

> I hope it will help him gain their full acceptance. After the final Celtic game of the season, fans were very disappointed and a number of them called for his head. I didn't subscribe to that view and I thought he at least deserved one more season – that has been proved. It may have been unexpected but we won the SPL on merit.

However, Elaine Sommerville, for one, will take some persuading:

> I think most Rangers supporters aren't happy with Alex McLeish and would like a higher-profile boss. If we hadn't won the league I think a lot of them would be calling for him to go. I thought there was an improvement this season so I'm willing to give him more time to see if that continues next season. My main concern is our tactics in Europe; I have still to be convinced he has what it takes to allow us to progress there.

And what about the forgotten Advocaat, from whom the luckless McLeish had to pick up the pieces that cold December day in 2001? Jim Templeton offers an interesting view: 'For eighteen months it was a disaster but in ten years time he will be talked about as a brilliant manager.'

THE CONTRIBUTORS

Alex Anderson

Born in North Ayrshire thirty-six years ago, Alex Anderson's first football love was Ardrossan Winton Rovers. However, on 2 April 1977, the junior Alex made his senior spectating debut from the benches of the old centenary stand at Ibrox. Rangers defeated Hibernian 2–1 and his main memory of the game is refusing to cheer when Jock Wallace's side equalised. 'I only deigned to get off my seven-year-old backside when we eventually took the lead. A natural bluenose!' Alex is co-author, with Ronnie Esplin, of two books on Rangers: *Barcelona Here We Come* (Argyll, 2002) and *The Advocaat Years* (Argyll, 2004). He has also penned pieces for such varied publications as *When Saturday Comes*, *FourFourTwo*, *The Guardian* and the Dumbarton FC match programme. He lives in Glasgow with his wife and spends hours each week posting unnecessarily long articles on the website, *Rangers.OpenFootball.co.uk*.

Colin Armstrong

Colin was born a stone's throw away from Ibrox Stadium in Glasgow's Southern & General Hospital in March, 1973; ten months after the European Cup Winners' Cup had been secured in Barcelona. Taking his forename from his father's favourite player, Colin Stein, his first game was around season 1980/81 when he witnessed a home match against Morton. Colin is currently a civil servant with the Inland Revenue but has written for a variety of publications in the past. He was a columnist for both *Rangers News* and the matchday programme and has also worked for publications such as *When Saturday Comes* and *Pride of Scotland* magazine.

Currently studying journalism at Cardonald College, Colin lives with his wife Shona and their baby son, Connor, in Falkirk. A season-ticket holder in the Copland rear, his ambition is that Rangers will one day challenge consistently in the European arena.

Gavin Berry

Born in Glasgow, Gavin started out in journalism at *Rangers News*, covering the youth and reserve teams before moving onto first-team affairs. He helped launch *Rangers Monthly* magazine and then the club's official website prior to his move to the *Sunday Mail* in the summer of 2002. He picked up the prestigious Jim Rodger memorial award for 2004 when he was voted Scotland's Young Sportswriter of the Year.

Ronnie Esplin

Ronnie was managing editor of Guildford-based Arena Leisure's football website in the nineties before returning north of the border to become a freelance sports writer.

While filing mainly for the Press Association, his work also appears in various national newspapers such as *Scotland on Sunday*, *Sunday Times*, *Sunday Mirror*, *The Times* and the *Scottish Mirror* as well as on several sporting websites.

As well as being a regular feature writer for *FourFourTwo* magazine, Ronnie is also author of, *Down the Copland Road* (Argyll, 2000) and co-writer of both, *Barcelona Here We Come* (Argyll, 2002) and *The Advocaat Years* (Argyll, 2004).

Colin Glass

Colin was born in Dundee, and attended his first Rangers match over forty years ago, when his older sister, a Dundee United fan, took him to see the Gers record a 3–1 victory at Tannadice. Colin left Dundee in 1975 to take up a full-time position at Rangers Pools, then the largest pools operation run by a football club in the world, before pursuing a successful career in financial services from 1979 to 2002. In 2003 he was one of the founders of the Rangers Supporters Trust and became its first chairman. Colin is married with two grown-up daughters, the elder of whom still occupies the seat next to him in the club deck at Ibrox. His first Old Firm match was the Ibrox Disaster game, and he exited that fateful day down stairway 13, fortunately before disaster struck. Colin says that his greatest ambition is 'to see Rangers win the Champions League' – a day that *really* would shake the football world!

Lisa Gray

Lisa had aspirations of working as a magazine journalist when she graduated from Cardonald College with an HND in Journalism at the age of nineteen but ambitions of writing for *Vogue* and *Marie Claire* were swapped for Saturday afternoons spent at football grounds around Scotland instead. Her first game as a reporter was Partick Thistle on a wet and windy Tuesday night for the *Daily Record*. She later went on to contribute to the *Scottish Mirror* before joining the Press Association as a sports reporter in May 2000. Lisa was born in Glasgow.

Scott McDermott

Scott grew up in Castlemilk, Glasgow and still lives there today. He played youth football with Dundee and Partick Thistle before achieving an honours degree in media theory and production at Paisley University. In 2000, he reported on lower league Scottish football for the *Daily Record* before moving to the *Scottish Mirror* to cover the Premier League on a freelance basis. In 2002, Scott was accepted on to the Donald Dewar Scholarship Scheme at the *Daily Record* and *Sunday Mail* and as part of the course had spells at the *Hamilton Advertiser*, *The Glaswegian* and the *Daily Record* news desk. At the same time Scott was undertaking freelance sports reporting for the *Sunday Mail* and after sixteen months of the Dewar Scheme, he started full time on the *Mail's* sports desk, contributing to the paper and the *Mailsport Weekly* magazine.

Robert McElroy

Robert is a freelance writer who has spent many years researching the history of Rangers. He is editor and publisher of *The Rangers Historian* magazine, and his previous books on the club include *Rangers Player by Player* (Crowood Press, 1990; updated Hamlyn editions 1997 and 1998); *Rangers Season by Season* (True Blue Publications, 1992), *Rangers – The Complete Record* (Breedon Books, 1996), *Rangers Images 1872–1964*, (Tempus Publishing, 1998) and *The Spirit of Ibrox* (Lancaster Publishing, 1999).

A Glaswegian by birth and inclination, and a keen student of both political and sporting history, he believes that the growth and development of Rangers Football Club from the humble origins of the public pitches on Glasgow Green to the multi-million pound business of today deserves recognition as one of the great romantic stories of world sport.

Graham Walker

Graham was born and raised in Glasgow and has been a Rangers supporter for over forty years. He is currently professor of politics at Queen's University, Belfast. He has authored and edited several books on Scottish and Irish history and politics.

His publications and articles include: *A History of the Ulster Unionist Party: Protest, Pragmatism and Pessimism* (Manchester University Press, 2004); 'Identity questions in contemporary Scotland: faith, football and future prospects', *Contemporary British History* Volume 15, no.11 (spring 2001); and *A Biographical Dictionary of British Prime Ministers* (Routledge, 1998), co-edited with B. Eccleshall.

Chris Williamson

A native of east Belfast, 24-year-old Chris Williamson has supported Rangers for as long as he can remember. Chris graduated from the University of Stirling in 2003, and plies his trade as a freelance sports writer and reporter. He is a regular features contributor to *Total Football* magazine in his homeland and has covered numerous international youth tournaments, including the 2005 FIFA World Youth Championships, on behalf of *topdrawersoccer.com*.